Lord, Help Me . . . I Have A Date!

Samuel H. Hancock Ed.D.

WESTBOW
PRESS®
A DIVISION OF THOMAS NELSON
& ZONDERVAN

Scripture taken from the King James Version of the Bible.

WestBow Press books may be ordered through booksellers or by contacting:

WestBow Press
A Division of Thomas Nelson & Zondervan
1663 Liberty Drive
Bloomington, IN 47403
www.westbowpress.com
1 (866) 928-1240

ISBN: 978-1-9736-2663-3 (sc)
ISBN: 978-1-9736-2664-0 (e)

Print information available on the last page.

WestBow Press rev. date: 05/06/2018

Dedication

This book is dedicated to my wife, Kattie Hancock, who is and has always been, in addition to God, my source of inspiration. Without her love, support, encouragement, patience, and simply being the wonderful, selfless person she is, this book would have never become a reality. Thank you, honey, for allowing me to share our love story with the world.

Contents

Chapter Summaries

Chapter I: The importance of knowing yourself; dealing with "first date" anxiety questions; using dating metaphorically as driving a car; the H.A.L.T. effect.

Chapter II: A discussion about dealing with the times in your life when you are "under construction," how life issues can have you "driving in circles" and a few suggestions for making yourself more attractive.

Chapter III: An example of how God is the ultimate matchmaker, a true story about a match "not made in heaven" and some suggestions which could help you connect with the "right" person.

Chapter IV: The importance of slowing down during the dating journey, being patient, children, money, step-parenting, trust and the S.L.O.W. effect.

Chapter V: A discussion about Online and Long Distance dating.

Chapter VI: Flirting, dating in the Church and a case study about how dating between two members of the same Church unfolded.

Introduction

D o you remember your first date? How about your first car? I am sure you remember both. My first car was a 1963 Buick, and it was a piece of junk. I was advised not to purchase it, and it lasted about six months. But my first date was great. She was cute, I liked her a lot, and I remember spending all my paper route money on her. The point is, I remember them both very well. One experience was rocky, but the other one was a lot smoother. That's one reason why I compare dating to purchasing a new car. Before you can drive a car, you need to know the basics: where to put the key, how to turn on the lights and windshield wipers, how to adjust the seat and rearview mirror, and the like. And reading the Operator's Manual might not be a bad idea. You ever heard of a dating manual?

In 1960 Chevrolet introduced an automobile into the market place called the Corvair. The automobile got twenty-nine miles to the gallon—twice that of any other car on the road at that time—had a rear-drive engine, was compact, and was touted as revolutionary. However, when a revolution occurs, there are always casualties. And it was no different with the Corvair. The design of the automobile was flawed because of the unequal distribution of the car's weight, which created instability and "exerted a spin-out force like that of an ice-skater on the end of a crack-the-whip line." After millions of dollars in lawsuits and a significant number of fatalities and injuries, production of the Corvair ceased. This automobile was destined to fail because of its design. It did not matter how good it looked, how fast it drove, how many miles per gallon it got, or how much its designers wanted it to work. Relationships, particularly in the context of dating, ironically seem to unfold in the same way. If the design—the blueprint or foundation—is flawed, the relationship will be unstable and fraught with problems, will not work properly, and will ultimately fail. Dating is hard enough as it is. Why make it harder because of a flawed or shaky foundation?

Thanks to the internet, reality TV, and the highly sexualized society that we live in, our world is barraged with hundreds, maybe thousands, of stories daily about male-female relationships. Many are entertaining, most are interesting and, of course, a significant number are tragic. I am hoping that something I share in this book will not only provide those who are dating with new insights but also enhance the quality of male-female relationships in general. The collateral damage that often occurs when relationships end badly or marriages collapse can be devastating. Hopefully, some of my thoughts, ideas, and recommendations can provide you with direction, encouragement, and peace during this season in your life.

Preface

When I started dating following the death of my spouse after more than thirty years of marriage, I realized there were very few people to talk with about what I was experiencing. Although I have since remarried, I became aware that as a widower, I was grieving and I would need to allow some time to elapse before I would start to feel some semblance of normalcy. However, I simply did not know what to expect or what pitfalls I needed to be aware of. In other words, I could have benefited from the advice of someone with some insight into what I was experiencing. Although I had four siblings who were single and whom I loved and respected, each of them lived in another city, and none of them seemed very interested in dating or remarrying. Each of them had been married previously, but each had also been divorced at least twice (except for one). They were not exactly experts when it came to giving their younger brother dating or relationship advice. My parents were deceased, and I could not talk to my friends because they we were all married.

It did not take long for me to realize that when my pastor (and most pastors) talked with parishioners from the pulpit, they told stories, joked, or gave advice in the context of marriage. Why? Because, most pastors were married, and a significant number of their parishioners were also married. I don't even think many of them were aware of this because, as a pastor, it is their responsibility to address the needs of those in their congregation. Nonetheless, I started feeling really left out and even lonelier. In addition, I had always known that most married men were not exactly excited about a single man having conversations with their wives. Also, the thought of me as a single man keeping company with married men regularly could have been a problem as well. Their interests and mine were a little different from a relationship perspective. I knew other single men whom I had befriended over the years. Yet going to the movies, to dinner, or to sporting events with another man was simply not appealing to me. As a matter of fact, one single man I knew told me that he did not have a girlfriend, did not need a girlfriend, and did not want a girlfriend. I suspect that no woman wanted him, but that's another story. Singles are sometimes a forgotten group, particularly in the church, because most church leaders are—what? Married!

Our friends can sometimes unwittingly make the journey even more difficult. For example, when singles are seen with members of the opposite sex, some friends tend to assume that the relationship is romantic in nature, as opposed to a friendship. Also, if you're seen together more than once, then you are *definitely* dating. Sometimes all you want is someone to talk to. Singles must be careful not to allow others to make them feel like they should *own* the values, opinions, attitudes, and patterns of thinking that belong to others.

The idea of finding a book on dating joining a support group was foreign to me, so I just floundered. At times I was on an emotional rollercoaster, and I needed a roadmap to navigate the sensitive terrain of understanding the human transaction in the context of dating. In some ways I was my own worst enemy. I didn't take the advice I received from a single woman who had been a friend for over thirty years. I still thought I could make good decisions. Why wouldn't I? I always had. Little did I know that I did not *know* what I did not *know*. If I had known what I did not know then, I might have avoided some of the mistakes I made with my time, money, and emotions. A book of this nature could not only have helped me avoid some of those mistakes, but it could also have given me some insight into why I was feeling the way I was about what I was going through. I might have made the same decisions anyway. Yet, if someone I knew and trusted had given me a book to read that helped me on my journey, I would really have appreciated it. Maybe you know someone who has "kissed dating goodbye," someone who has recently exited a painful relationship, or someone who simply could use some guidance in dealing with the phenomenon that we refer to as "dating."

It is my desire that you can benefit from reading this book, or maybe you can help someone you know who falls into one of the following four categories:

- Never married: If you would like to find a mate, this book will provide you with an itinerary for starting the journey.
- Divorced: This book will provide you with insight into what you should look out for while you evaluate dating and/or lifelong partner candidates.
- Widower: This book will provide you with insight into what to expect while grieving and how to deal with issues that will surface during the dating process.
- Widow: This book will help you avoid mistakes that some widows make during the early stages of dating and also provide you with insight concerning the dating process.

It is my hope and prayer that the information contained in this book will be a blessing to you and will help someone work though some of the issues with which I struggled.

Acknowledgements

The first person I must thank is my Lord and Savior Jesus Christ for creating me, sustaining me, and for just being the good God that he is. I must thank my wife, Kattie, who is my best friend and my ultimate sounding board. I would like to thank Dr. Karen Patterson Stewart for her encouragement, suggestions, and for being a friend; my pastor, the Reverend Dr. John E. Roberts, for being an awesome inspirational leader; and all of my children—Sam, Arnold, Seccoya, Lawrence, Amy, Trent and Nina—just for growing up to be decent, hardworking, mature adults. Thanks to Dr. Linda Whittington Clark for being a friend, confidante, and colleague; Opal Bacon for her editing skills; my sister-in-law Cynthia Ball for proofreading the manuscript; Bishop Dr. Marjorie Holt; Dr. Brehon Hall; author Theresa Braddy; Rita Bell; the singles ministries at the Indiana Avenue Missionary Baptist Church; my church family for your prayers; and the singles ministries at the Friendship Missionary Baptist Church in Columbus, Ohio.

After I completed my doctoral studies in 2005, I counted the number of people who helped me, and I stopped at thirty. After I completed this book and started counting the number of people who helped me, I stopped at fifty. As a result, if you assisted me in any way, shape, or form, I thank you very, very much.

Foreword

"Good book! It is one of a kind to assess your present ability to love and be loved as well as prepare you for a great rewarding godly life with a God-given mate that has been under construction and made just for you! A very relevant release!"

- Bishop Marjorie Holt, publisher, founder,
and owner of the Interfaith Gazette

Dr. Samuel Hancock in this work, *Lord Help Me . . . I Have a Date*, has given the body of Christ at large a swift kick that it has needed for some time! He has scholarly penned a masterpiece to help those maintain integrity while saved, single, satisfied, and seeking. This book is a must read for those who are contemplating dating again, and those who currently are. The discussion of dating is a conversation that has been taboo in the church spectrum until now. This will serve as tool for single ministries across the length and breadth of this world!

- Bishop Brehon Hall pastor of New Psalmist Church

"Hello, hello . . . I'm sorry, you must have called the wrong number" is *not* the way to avoid a potential invitation to go out on a first date because you've suddenly got cold feet! Dr. Samuel H. Hancock has brilliantly composed a masterpiece on reentering the dating scene for the "mature" audience. Many issues prevent people from taking the next step, returning to the dating scene after the end of a relationship. Dr. Hancock coaches you through the delicate steps maintaining the central issue at the forefront: *God first!* I have known Dr. Hancock since 1971. He is a professional who is grounded in his faith.

Our paths have crossed professionally in several areas: service providers in the community, educators at The University of Toledo, therapists in a private practice, and community choral and church activities. In all areas Dr. Hancock has proven to be a servant for the Lord. He is highly respected and revered by his church, our peers, and in the professional community.

For years, Dr. Hancock, has helped and inspired people from all walks of life. His advice assists persons to live a victorious life. He will guide you to a joyful and fulfilling, quality relationship!

- Dr. Linda Whittington Clark Licensed Counseling Psychologist, Founder and Owner of Whittington Clark and Associates LLC

Chapter I

Do You Know How to Drive?

One rainy, summer evening just about dusk, I had picked up a few photographs which I'd had developed, and I was feeling good. Then I saw the text on my cell phone. It was from a young lady I had been seeing and it announced that "it was over." She was not feeling very good about me and had decided to move on . . . with no warning. It's very interesting to look at the sky right before nightfall, because at times it looks a little grayish, not black or white, just grayish . . . very vague. The text message coupled with the rain made me feel lost, alone, and very insignificant. Life seemed to be very "vague" as well. It was not clear to me what direction I should go in. Although we had not been seeing each other that long, I really felt good about the relationship and thought we were headed in the right direction . . . I had not seen this coming. I really liked her. Before I knew it, I started to weep softly. I could not believe it. Did I really like her that much? Maybe I did . . . but what really hurt was simply being rejected . . . I was not ready for that . . . I had done a poor job of protecting my heart.

Knowing and understanding yourself and knowing how secure you are is a lot like knowing the overall condition of your automobile. Is there oil in the engine? Are the tires in good condition? When was the last time you had a tune-up? Is your car in shape to travel? Knowing what your values, attitudes, and beliefs are is like knowing if your car is ready for the road. You may not know how long or difficult the journey may be. But if your automobile (mind, body, and soul) is not ready for the journey, you are in for a rocky ride. That rainy summer day in 2008 made me realize I was *not ready* for the ride!

Are you ready for the journey?

One way to look at starting the dating journey is to compare it to how you feel when you begin to learn how to drive. You must demonstrate that you can operate a vehicle before being issued a driver's license, and you need to have the *confidence* that you can handle a motor vehicle. A certain level of *maturity* is required to take on such a major responsibility, and you need good dexterity, eyesight, and peripheral vision so you can see your blind spots while driving.

You need those same skills on the highway of life before you can earn and be awarded a "dating license." Of course, once you start traveling on this highway for the first time, you will experience a certain amount of nervousness or anxiety, particularly, if you are attracted to the person. And, as you probably know, attraction is a key prerequisite for going out on a date with this person in the first place.

Whether or not the person is someone you are thinking about dating exclusively, your comfort level in having these discussions at all will be directly related to whether you are ready. These discussions can also be called "speed bumps" because this part of the dating journey will probably be uncomfortable and will force you to slow down. Therefore, it is important that you know if you are positioned to date. What does being "positioned" mean? Let me explain. Do you have a Global Positioning System (GPS)? Most people do in one form or another. It is a wonderful tool for guiding you to your destination, and you depend on this tool so much that you don't even think about how you are going to get from A to B. You put your destination in the GPS. Very simple. However, what many of you do not know is that if the satellite that feeds the GPS does not contain accurate information, your GPS can have you going in circles. This happens primarily when road construction has occurred and the satellite has not been sent updated information. Some of you may have experienced this phenomenon. I know I have.

Consequently, it is crucial that you make sure that you still know how to read a map, or you won't know how to reach your destination. Unfortunately, the brain, which works like a computer, has a ton of information in it, like a satellite that feeds your internal GPS that you depend on to lead you in the right direction. Yet often the landscape of life has changed drastically, and roads you have traveled previously or courses of action you have taken in the past that have been stored in that computer brain are now either under construction, closed, or have been detoured into an unfamiliar area. In your haste to reach your destination quickly, you need to pull over (self-awareness) and *read the map*, because otherwise you really won't know how to get to where you're going. Another way to look at the GPS is to understand that if you put in the wrong information—which could result from a lack of self-awareness—you will not know how to locate the right person because you won't be headed in the right direction.

Who is that right person? It will be very difficult to know what kind of person you want or need in your life. What are your interests, values, beliefs? It would be easy if all you had to do was choose between a low-down, no good, chauvinist (if you're a woman) or gold-digger (if you're a man) and a wonderful person. But of course, it's never that easy. Most of the time, you are choosing between two, three, or more attractive opportunities for love.

The problem is that the dating highway is littered with cover-up artists. I'll call them "insincere daters" with smiles on their faces, compliments coming out of their mouths, and adoring eyes that look at you like you are the be all and end all. For a time, they're on their best behavior. Unfortunately, after a while, these cover-up artists shed their masks. Smiles disappear, and those compliments change to hurtful barbs. Those adoring eyes are now looking for what they *think* you have instead of who you are.

If you are smart, you will end relationships with these selfish people and accept and endure the pain that comes with a breakup. However, the better alternative is to develop the wisdom to discern good choices for dating from bad ones before the investment of time and heart. Who you date is a critical decision because the more time you spend with a person, the more likely your feelings will be involved. Developing discernment can help you avoid the pitfalls of dating the wrong people. It all starts with your relationship with God. *"Seek ye first the Kingdom of God and all these things will be added unto you - Matt 6:33.*

It is important that, once you know who you are, you become secure in who you are, know where you are going, and develop some insight into where you have been. Before you can really talk about yourself and your past or future, you must be prepared to have that discussion. Like the GPS, you need to know your current location before you can get to where you are going. For example, do you really believe you can handle having a master's degree and dating a blue-collar worker? Have you even thought about it? Are you ready to talk about it? Where are you spiritually? Have you really thought about it?

Naturally, you are probably not going to allow such intellectualism to be in control on a first date. Other thoughts are running rampant and you are more concerned with things like: *Will he like me? Will I like her? Does he think I am cute? Does she think I am fine? What should I wear? Oh, I can't wear that! That makes me look fat!! Is he going to be weird? Will he think I am weird? Where should we go? Maybe we should try lunch first? He looks like the last date I had in 2001 (and I am still single). Is he the one? How much is it going to cost me to find out?*

These are called *first date anxiety questions,* and I am sure you have experienced them just as I have. Questions about what to wear, what to talk about, and how to combat shyness may ignite an anxious mind. You need to first understand that anxiety is a natural part of life. You will experience some degree of worry in your life, and single people experience anxiety around dating, relationships, and commitment, so a first date with a stranger can feel like an insurmountable task. It is important to remember that some anxiety is reasonable and realistic to expect. It is human nature to be nervous in a new situation with a new person. Knowing who you are and developing insight into what you are going through at this stage in your life is crucial.

Here are a few suggestions for dealing with first date anxiety:

- Avoid labeling anxious thoughts, feelings, and sensations as bad or perceiving them in a self-defeating way. Some of the most common anxious thoughts that you might have when you think about dating are: *My date doesn't like me, or I will be boring.* A significant number of people tend to predict that negative things will happen to them in the future and try to read other people's minds. Resist the urge to try to figure out what others are thinking.
- Remember that anxious thoughts breed anxious thoughts, so break the cycle by taking a step back, reminding yourself that your anxiety will pass, and replacing an anxious thought with something more positive.
- Plan out several conversation starters or topics for the date. What are you confident talking about? Which subjects are interesting to you? What can you teach your date? Having a plan is helpful.

The key to managing dating anxiety is to resist allowing it to control you, hijack your date, or prevent you from dating if it is love that you are looking for. If you view dating as an entertaining experience with normal ups and downs, you will put less pressure on yourself. In addition, if you view dating as an exciting adventure or exploration, feel that you are deserving of love, and believe that you will find the right person in time, your anxiety level is also likely to decrease.

When you begin the journey of entering a relationship with a person of the opposite sex, you may think that you know yourself, and you do on some level. But before you can determine what you are looking for in a partner, you need to devote a significant amount of time to thinking about your attitudes, standards of conduct, and values. You must also examine your patterns of thinking, attitudes, and overall belief system. Until you conduct that kind of assessment, your view of a person you might be interested in dating will be distorted because that view will be based on incomplete data resulting from an incomplete self-assessment. You could be making decisions based on what's pleasing to the eyes (Job 31:1), not on what is pleasing to God, based on an examination of yourself that is not as thorough as it could be.

For example, since I am a man, I know that a man may tell himself repeatedly that this particular woman is "the one" after getting her anatomy in his line of sight. The flesh will make decisions for you every chance that it gets, and as a Christian man, you need to become acutely aware of the need to suppress that part of yourself (Romans 6:11), and work toward imitating Jesus (Ephesians 5:1) and living worthy of your calling (Philippians 1:27). Suffice it to say that if you are a man, you take in a lot of information through your eyes, and frequently your thoughts can be easily dominated by publications like *Hustler* and *Playboy* that tend to distort your thinking even more. These magazines exploit a woman's anatomy in a graphic way. You might be wondering why these magazines would be attractive to a Christian man. You might be saying to yourself that a Christian man would never read this kind of material. Yet, according to an online survey of nearly 3,000 adults teenagers and pastors by the Barna Research group most pastors have struggled with pornography in the past and in the present. The study included 432 pastors and 338 youth pastors and revealed that 57% of the pastors surveyed and 64% of the youth pastors admitted that they have had problems in this area.

You just need to be *aware* of your deficiencies. Of course, women are not exempt from allowing what's pleasing to the eyes to create problems (*Playgirl*, male strip clubs).

Now, ladies, when you meet a guy who's either very handsome or who is cute, well dressed, well built, and a great listener, you will naturally become interested, but that is when you need to H-A-L-T. You tend to make your biggest mistakes in life when you are either <u>H</u>ungry (for food or for a relationship), <u>A</u>ngry, <u>L</u>onely, or <u>T</u>ired. Therefore, you need to HALT and let God, through the Holy Spirit, talk to you. I think that is one reason why it's so easy for a guy to pick up a woman at bars, taverns, parties, or anywhere that alcohol is served.

Think about it. You might be lonely, or after a few drinks you could find yourself hungry for food or companionship. As a result, and because alcohol acts initially as a stimulant (though it is ultimately a depressant), fatigue occurs much more quickly and your inhibitions drop. You behave in abnormal ways or you just say, "Why not?" It is important to *know yourself* and your limits, when to recognize danger zones, and when you are most vulnerable. I realize the thought that Christians don't drink or go to taverns crosses your mind, and of course you should absolutely refrain from such activities (Ephesians 5:18, 4:1). But unfortunately, some of your brothers and sisters do, in fact, drink occasionally and probably excessively more than they want to admit. You might not go to a tavern, but how about a cabaret or a house party?

Walking close with the Lord can help you work through these issues, but they are issues that you need to be aware of. With God's help, you will be able to use the spirit of discernment to help you manage the impact these issues may have on your body, mind, soul, and spirit during your Christian walk (Romans 12:2; Hosea 14:9).

Okay. The first date is over. Mission accomplished. Now you allow your reasoning ability, along with the help of God, to assist you in processing the experience and to provide you with wisdom. If the date was disappointing, you try to determine why. Maybe the conversation was difficult with a lot of pauses, or the movie you went to see was as boring as you felt he or she *thought* you were. Maybe you could try another venue such as a sporting event or a concert, if there's mutual interest. Evaluate it and avoid the extremes of "it was the most awful dating experience from. . . ." (you know where) and now you are off to the cloister, or "it was the most wonderful, fantastic date I have ever been on and I know I am in love." The bottom line is you did it, you lived through it, and now you can now focus on the dating journey. Lord, help me. I'm dating!

Chapter II

Road Ahead Is under Construction

Road Hazard

How many times have you seen this sign? Now answer this question. How many times have you seen this sign and ignored it? Think about it. Sometimes when you see this sign, you think that *maybe* the constructions is over and they forgot to take the sign down, or the construction is not that severe and you will probably be okay. In other words, you fail to *prepare* yourself for the fact (or at least the distinct possibility) that you may encounter a delay in your journey. Sometimes you might not even reduce your speed. "Under construction" means just what it says, incomplete or unfinished. Of course, none of us will ever really be finished, as we will always be a work in progress (Philippians 3:14). However, if you are a widow, widower, divorcee, or someone who has never been married, and has ended a relationship, you would probably agree, to some extent, that you are "under construction." Road construction takes time and you, as a traveler, must be patient with the process because you want the work to be done right. If you drive fifty miles an hour through a construction zone where the posted signs read ten miles an hour, you might run into some problems.

This journey you are on called "life" is no different. You must read the signs and allow the reconstruction of your life, and the life of the person you are with, to unfold at its own pace because when the work is finished, the pavement of life will be smoother, more attractive, safer, and long-lasting. Think for a moment about how it feels to drive on new pavement, nice and fresh with easy-to-see yellow or white lines, wider lanes, better lighting, and improved landscaping. You don't want to admit it, but you will say to yourself privately that it was worth the wait. It was a process and to a certain extent still is. Every year orange barrels appear everywhere, and you wonder if construction will ever be finished. Sometimes the construction frightens you, particularly when you drive at night. How many of you love driving between two concrete walls that create a narrow corridor that's twenty or thirty miles long? If you are not an experienced driver, or even if you are, dealing with that kind of construction can make you very fearful about traveling.

The Road to Feeling Secure

People have one basic need which requires two kinds of input for its satisfaction. The most basic need is a sense of personal worth, the acceptance of oneself as a whole, real person. The two required qualities are significance (purpose, importance, adequacy for a job, meaningfulness, impact) and security (love, unconditional and consistently expressed). You need to feel like you belong, have value, and are competent. If you feel like you belong, you feel accepted; if you feel you have value, you feel loved; and if you feel like you are competent, you feel secure. There's that word again, *secure*.

I was fortunate enough to be a passenger on the Tom Joyner Morning Show Fantastic Voyage in 2009, and I participated in a sixty-second sales contest hosted by Jay Anthony Brown and sponsored by Home Depot. They asked for volunteers and each participant was required to make a sales pitch within sixty seconds about our respective businesses. I had a consulting firm at the time, and I had one minute to give the who, what, when, where, and how about my business. The winner received an all-expense paid trip to the National Supplier Diversity Conference in New Orleans in October of that year. By the time I entered, the line of participants had grown to at least a dozen people in front of me. However, after each one gave a sales pitch, I gave mine and was selected as a co-winner of the trip to New Orleans. I would not have had the nerve, self-confidence, or courage to enter this contest, let alone be competitive in selling myself, two or three years earlier. Why? Because I did not know myself, and . I needed to develop more self-confidence and become more secure before I could project a confident image to others. It was a process.

Getting Lost Trying to Leave Detroit

One of the biggest problems you might have is that you really think you know where you are going or, I might add, you are simply lost and *don't know it.* I live about sixty miles from Detroit, Michigan, and I have traveled there at least a hundred times. I had never had any problems entering or exiting the city. However, between 2007 and 2009, major highway and road construction was taking place in Detroit, and many familiar exit and entrance ramps had been closed, changed, or detoured. What made matters even worse was that, in most instances, the original signs had not been removed or covered up. As a result, I might think an exit was open, but it really wasn't. I wouldn't realize it until I had actually started toward the exit. Now, to Detroit's credit, on most of the signage they would put the word "detour" or the name of another exit you could take that would get you to Interstate 75. Unfortunately, it would just become even more confusing. So what I decided to do was to pull over and put my home address in my GPS. I just knew the GPS would get me home. Nonetheless, because of the construction, the satellite which drives the GPS had not been updated, so the GPS had me literally going in circles because it was confused as well. Without accurate information, the GPS could not give me proper directions. Sound familiar?

This real-life example seems a little humorous because I probably sound like I am logistically challenged. I know my wife thinks I am. Yet, what if you find yourself going in circles late at night and you are running low on fuel? What if you are in the wrong part of town and you are afraid of making a wrong turn? Detroit is no different from most large cities. Some parts of town should probably be avoided, particularly if you're alone late at night. This happened to me more than once. Consequently, I quit going to Detroit until that construction was over. I was tired of getting lost, and I also knew that until I could secure accurate information, I would continue to run the risk of getting lost. As much as I enjoyed being in Detroit, the problems I encountered on the journey were not worth it, and I had to accept the fact that I was not ready for the trip.

Dating, in many respects, is the same way. In addition, driving down the same street repeatedly can become boring and frustrating. You need to take a different route and look for new ways to meet people. It's similar to driving on an unfamiliar road at night. Ideally, you would like to be able to see the whole route before you begin, but instead you see it progressively. As you move forward, a little more of the road is revealed. Sometimes you need to drive slowly so you can see your way more clearly.

If events that have occurred in your life have made it difficult, if not impossible, for you to enjoy feelings of security, purpose, meaningfulness, significance, joy, worth, and competence, discussing how those events have helped to shape who you are with someone with whom you are developing a serious relationship can be a problem. Therefore, before you can discuss your past, you must be *prepared* to have that discussion. How much thought have you given to some of the areas outlined in the preceding discussion? A significant number of men generally struggle with talking about their feelings, and if you're a man and you're reading this, you need to ask yourself a question: *What aspects of my life do I find difficult to discuss, if any?*

Using my experiences as a widower as an example, on the anniversary of my late wife's passing, I was visiting another city and waiting for a young lady I had been dating to return from an errand. I found myself suddenly feeling extremely depressed and lonely. Thirty years of marriage to a woman you believe was always truthful with you and being her caregiver for several years has a way of making you feel both needed and important. As the young lady I was visiting was running very late, I went through a few stages of abandonment (anger, hurt, disappointment), and when she did return, I lashed out at her and threatened to get a cab and leave town. I was still in the early stages of the mourning process and did not realize it.

Fortunately, I was able to work through it. But the point is that I did not realize what I was going through. I simply was unaware. In retrospect, I don't think that I was in the right frame of mind to manage the challenges associated with being in a relationship, and I was not feeling very secure or confident. It has been said that there are no problem marriages. There are just two people who have premarital issues, and when they marry, those issues collide. If you don't make a concerted effort to address these issues during the dating process, they will surface later and be much more difficult to address.

A Young Couple's Journey

I was counseling a young couple who said they were Christians, and they were talking about a variety of issues with which they had been struggling. However, they constantly complained about what I will call "residual" (baby mama drama, child support) issues from his last marriage, from his childhood, and the like that he maintained were the primary reasons he was struggling in his current marriage. I told him that our past does have an impact on our future, but does not *dictate* our future. That's our responsibility with the help of the Holy Spirit. I told him that if he continued to make his past experiences an *excuse* for problems in his current marriage, he would be destined to *always* have problems in interpersonal relationships because he could not change the past or the future. He could only deal with the here and now.

I reminded him that he needed to be *prepared* to examine himself and be ready to accept the fact that conversations he needed to have with his wife could be very painful, lengthy, and emotional, but necessary. Discussing what type of parenting a prospective mate received could be at a minimum uncomfortable, but essential. It is very important to discuss any molestation, incest, or other criminal behavior which may have occurred within one's family of origin and what impact it had on your prospective mate.

How Do You Define Attractiveness?

The first rule of dating is attraction. A person must be attractive to you and you to them. One of the mistakes that people make is settling for someone they "really like," and in some cases might love, but are not attracted to. I am sure most pastors can cite example after example of couples they have counseled over the years who have had serious marital problems. Sometimes these problems stemmed from the realization, perhaps after years of marriage, that at least one of them was never attracted to the other. Before a man or woman can really know what is attractive to him or her, he or she must first *know* what physical attributes they value. Self-awareness is a lifelong process.

When you're attracted to another person, sometimes you can't even define what it is you like. But you know that you are attracted to the person. Although his or her physical attributes captured your attention initially, after you engage that person in a conversation, you usually begin noticing other attributes that you find pleasing. The way a person talks, the clothes the person wears, the way the person walks, their mannerisms, their smile, or the sound of their voice, and on to the various parts of their anatomy. You may think that you know what you like, but sometimes you fear you will not recognize the person God has chosen for you when he or she appears. Will you know that this is the one? That is understandable. But that is when you need to trust God (Proverbs 3:6). You need to trust and believe that God will show you what you need and tell you when this person is the right one.

Sometimes your frame of reference, particularly if you're in a long-term relationship or were married for a significant period of time, is directly related to that person. What I mean is that sometimes you consciously or subconsciously seek someone who reminds you of that other person. Of course, if there were problems in the relationship that led to divorce or another painful parting, you may have determined that you will never get involved with anyone like that person. However, if you're a widow or widower or if you were in a marriage that ended involuntarily on your part, you may, on some level, be looking for a person similar in physical appearance to your previous spouse. As a result, when you get such a person in your line of sight, you may be predisposed to be attracted to that person. This is why you need to be careful, as you may not be aware of why you feel the way you do toward that person. In your eagerness particularly men, to find someone who can end your feelings of loneliness, rejection, or thirst for companionship, you might mistake attraction for what is really familiarity. What you must resist is settling for someone for the wrong reasons.

You must be careful not to underestimate the importance of friendship and getting to know a person before you reach any conclusions about their attractiveness. As many of you have learned, being patient and taking time to get to know a person is essential because you may discover that, in some instances, what is on the inside of a person is what makes them beautiful on the outside. As we all know beauty is only "skin deep," and most of us were told by our parents that looks are not everything. However, a person's attractiveness does mean something. In addition, while you are defining attractiveness, you also need to take a good honest look at yourself. You may not be as attractive as you think you are. Do you consider yourself attractive? What attractive features do you have? If you don't know the answers to these questions, ask a close friend to give you an honest assessment. You might be surprised.

As men and women of God, you know that the word of God teaches that faith is the substance of things hoped for and the evidence of things not seen (Hebrews 11:1). You have also been taught that without faith it is impossible to please God, and that he is a rewarder of those who diligently seek. By faith you believe that your creator knows you better than anyone else and knows your heart. If you believe that he is omniscient (on everyone's mind), omnipresent (everywhere), and omnipotent (all powerful), why would you doubt that he would make a person available to you that you would find attractive?

The following are a few things you need to know about yourself and what you are looking for in a relationship.

- Do you know what you are looking for? If so, what is it? Someone just to spend time with or a prospective spouse?
- Have you thought about how long you should date someone before you start thinking about marriage? Are you comfortable telling a woman or a man what your intentions are at the beginning? Why or why not?
- Are you mentally, financially, and emotionally mature enough to handle a dating relationship? In other words, can you handle rejection? Do you know how to protect your money?
- Does the possibility of a long-term relationship frighten or intimidate you? Why or why not?
- How comfortable are you talking about sex?
- What do you know about dating? Do you think you know enough? If so, what do you know? If not, what do you need to know?
- How comfortable are you with disclosure? How much do you need to know about the person you are dating?
- Have you ever had a psychological assessment conducted on yourself? If not, how do you feel about this kind of instrument?

In addition, during this period of "construction," you should spend time enjoying the journey, having as much fun as you can, and avoiding self-pity and depression. Instead, use this time to improve your market value. Stepping out of your comfort zone and doing something different can be both challenging and intimidating. For example, let's write the word "attitude." Grab a pencil and draw two horizontal lines, one on the far left of a blank piece of paper and the other one on the far right. Now write the word "attitude" on the left line with your writing hand and write the same word on the right line with your other hand. When you look at the word written by the hand you do not write with, you see a picture of the kind of attitude we usually have when we are trying to do something new.

In a *Peanuts* cartoon, Charlie Brown says to Linus: "Perhaps you can give me an answer, Linus. What would you do if you felt that no one liked you?"

Linus replies, "I'd try to look at myself objectively and see what I could do to improve. That's *my* answer, Charlie Brown."

To which Charlie replies, "I hate that answer!"

There are a number of reasons that you might resist change like Charlie Brown. Change creates fear of the unknown, but our *attitude,* with the aid of the Holy Spirit, can help us control our fear (II Timothy 1:7). There are a number of reasons why you might, like Charlie Brown, resist change. Sometimes it's because the change is not self-initiated. When you lack ownership of an idea, you may resist it, even when it is in your best interest. You simply don't like the idea of being manipulated. Sometimes change makes you modify your habitual patterns and forces you to think, reevaluate, and sometimes unlearn past behavior. You like habits because they allow you to do things without much thought, which is why most of you have so many of them. First you form habits, but then your habits form you.

Investing in Yourself and Growing

While "under construction," don't forget to participate in social, recreational, cultural, and political events and learn how to connect with others. Developing yourself into a person who might be appealing to another person is like investing in the stock market or investing in your children, your family, or your career. If you expect to make a profit within a day, you are doomed! It is what you do day by day over the long haul that matters most. If you continue developing your people skills and letting your "assets" compound over time, the inevitable result is growth.

Although some of us are more gifted than others in making conversation, these kinds of skills can be learned and improved, but that process does not happen overnight. Having good people skills involves many facets, including but not limited to emotional intelligence, emotional strength, a sense of humor, ability to discuss a wide variety of topics, and a good sense of timing. If you have developed good skills in this area, it required quite a bit of seasoning for you to become the person that you are.

You might want to consider self-improvement projects such as:

- Body Image and Weight –Is there any need for change?
- Tone of Voice – How do I sound when I speak?
- Personality – Does it isolate me or draw me to others?
- Self-Esteem – Is too low, or am I secure?
- Emotional Intelligence – Can I handle my encounters in a mature way?
- Self-Affirmation – Do I need others to validate me?
- Interpersonal Communication Skills – Are my skills intact?
- Social Skills – Am I comfortable within a group setting?
- Recreational Skills – How do I enjoy myself when I'm alone?
- Professional Status – Am I satisfied with my profession? Am I in the right field?
- Education – Do I need more?
- Annual Income – Can I adequately take care of myself?
- Social Status – How do I feel about the people I am connected to in the community?
- Spirituality – Am I rooted and grounded in my faith?
- Financial Credit Status – What is my credit score?
- Home Environment – Is my home warm and inviting, or in need of repair?
- Transportation – Can I get around?
- Attractiveness –Am I satisfied with how I look?

The good news is that we can grow in the people skills area, regardless of our starting point. We simply need to be patient and allow these skills to develop. Take the story of Joseph. He was a cocky kid too arrogant for his own good. He did not think it was enough to be the favorite of his father, the child who received special treatment, the son of Jacob's old age; Joseph had to rub it in! When God sent Joseph a dream revealing that he would one day lead his family—not only his eleven brothers but his parents—Joseph thoughtlessly told everyone about it *twice*. His father rebuked him. His brothers wanted revenge, and they got it (Gen 37:1-11; 18-29). Early in life, Joseph did not know how to skillfully work with others. He lacked experience, wisdom, and humility, three qualities gained only with the passage of time. Joseph's life illustrates the law of process, which we can break down into phases.

The *first phase* is when you don't know what you don't know. Everyone starts in a state of ignorance, and that's where Joseph began. He did not understand the dynamics of his family. His brothers already hated him (Gen 37:3), and his ignorance cost him more than two decades of alienation from his family. Sometimes we don't know how much work it takes to develop skills in an area where we may be weak.

The *second phase*, you know what you don't know, might take a life-changing incident similar to the one that started Joseph on the road to change. When he was thrust into slavery, he came to understand and learn hard lessons in human nature and relationships. The process molded his character and taught him patience and humility. We may need to experience some pain, suffering, and disappointment such as setbacks in our career or missed opportunities to talk with colleagues and peers

The *third phase* involves knowing and growing, and here improvements start to show. You show great skill at interacting with others, and you shine only because you have paid the price of preparation. Joseph performed with excellence and great wisdom because he had paid the price for thirteen years.

With *phase four,* you simply go because of what you know.

Joseph's Journey

During seven years of plenty, Joseph executed his leadership plan with great skill. He was able to do that because of his maturity and the interpersonal skills he had developed. He filled the cities of Egypt with grain and prepared the country for a famine, but his true leadership manifested itself in the seven years following the famine. He not only fed the people of Egypt and other lands, but he also fulfilled the prophecy of his teenage years, when his developmental process began. Interpersonal skills need time to develop, but time alone cannot develop these skills. Some of us never experience this developmental stage and, as a result, never move through it.

Although nearly twenty-three years passed before he reunited with his family, Joseph realized that God had directed the process of his development. By the time his father died, Joseph had learned to see things from God's perspective, and when his brothers feared for their safety, he calmed them (Gen 50:19, 20). Joseph understood the long-term plan for his people, and it was a plan Joseph helped fulfill by growing into the leader God desired him to be. God wants all of us to develop the ability to reach out and witness to others, and that skill will help us in our personal life, particularly when we are looking for a mate.

Chapter III

Is This the Right Car for You?

Kattie and I had known each other for five or six years before we had our first date. Our spouses were still alive during the time she and I were working together on a community organizing committee. After our spouses passed away, a mutual friend of ours tried for over a year to arrange for us to go on a date together. I called her a few times, but she would never call me back. (I kid her about this all the time.) It was not God's will for us to meet (Phill 2:13), and I really don't think she or I were ready for each other.

When we eventually did have breakfast (she finally returned my phone call), we had a wonderful, comfortable, relaxing conversation, and the topic of her relationship with the Lord never came up. Quite frankly, it was not necessary for me to ask her about her relationship with the Lord. Why? Because, I had a strong feeling about the depth of her spirituality. It was not just because I had visited her church and seen her in service on several occasions, or that I knew her pastor. It also was not because she was a preacher, evangelist, or pastor. I was at peace and comfortable with her spiritually because I had observed her over the years in a variety of settings (church, community, and social). I had noticed how she carried herself, how she dressed, how she talked, and what she talked about. I knew she had a reputation for being a decent person, a person of high character and integrity. The fact that a couple of her relatives were also good Christian men and colleagues of mine didn't hurt. I had learned that just because a person is very involved in church does not mean that he or she is walking close with God. If a person has not consecrated himself or herself and you don't see on a daily basis a lifestyle is reflective of Christ (Romans 12:1-2), that kind of inconsistency will create serious problems within the relationship.

Each time I saw Kattie, our eyes would meet. Sometimes we would converse for only a few minutes, but every time I thought, "There is something different about this young lady," but I wasn't sure what it was. What is amazing to me is that prior to the breakfast, I had always seen Kattie in business and church attire, but I had never seen her dressed down in blue jeans. When I did, I said, "Wow!" That's when I became attracted to her.

The same thing had happened with Lorraine over thirty-five years prior to my breakfast with Kattie. Lorraine and I had dated for approximately a year and a half before we married. But about nine months before we married, she joined my church, got baptized, and both of us consecrated our lives and started living for the Lord. That is when we began the journey toward becoming equally yoked in our Christian walk. I knew that Lorraine and Kattie had a desire to serve the Lord, enjoyed worshiping, and that it would not be necessary for me to drag them to church. I knew that I was attracted to two women who would worship regularly with or without me, and that they had the kind of relationship with the Lord that would motivate them to talk to the Lord about what was bothering them, even if they were not interested in talking to me. If two people have the kind of relationship with the Lord that involves ongoing dialogue and faith that the Holy Spirit will guide them in the right direction (Proverbs 3:5-6), they will not only survive but, in most cases, will thrive.

Dating someone you are not equally yoked with can be compared to a devout Christian dating a Jehovah's Witness or a Muslim dating a devout Catholic. There is a difference between *saying* that you are Catholic, Jehovah's Witness, or Christian and practicing your beliefs. That's what I mean by devout. I am sure some relationships and marriages exist and thrive, even though the two are of a different faith, but I would contend that these relationships are the exception, not the rule.

A True Story . . .

A young man I know dated a woman for about six months, knowing that she was Catholic and that he was a devout Christian Baptist. He indicated that he really liked her and felt he was falling in love with her. He had met her through a mutual friend and was greatly attracted to her. In his words, she was fine! Their initial conversations were comfortable, and they connected right away. He was convinced that she probably was "the one." He said they really enjoyed each other's company, had many of the same interests, and their physical attraction was "electric." Nonetheless, they respected each other enough not to have sexual relations with each other while they were dating.

Yet, the relationship reached a crossroad when they were involved in a discussion about the fact that an item of a friend of hers was missing and that she needed to pray to Peter and Paul for the return of this item. Of course, my friend asked her why she thought Peter and Paul could restore this item. He said that he entered into a discussion with her about the word of God, and how he prayed to God the Father, the Son, and the Holy Spirit. It was during that conversation that the young lady revealed her belief in Catholicism and that she had been raised Catholic. She was still the same person that he had become very fond of, but he simply could not embrace her beliefs. Should they have had this discussion early in the relationship? Most definitely.

A conversation about faith does not need to occur on the first date. However, it should surface somewhere in the first few conversations with a person, and I think the best way to start the discussion is with a simple question: where do you worship? Any answer you receive will lead to some type of dialogue about faith. Why didn't this dialogue take place? Probably because other areas of mutual interest, as well as physical attraction, took precedent, which is not uncommon. Sometimes we convince ourselves that issues of faith will somehow work themselves out.

Whose responsibility was it to start the conversation about faith? It really does not matter which person introduces the topic, as long as someone does. Often it comes up naturally when you start talking about activities you enjoy participating in. Could things have been more complicated if they had gotten involved with each other sexually? Absolutely. Sexual sin is like no other sin because our sexuality bridges our body and soul. Although it is a physical act, it reaches beyond our physical body. The good thing about this situation was that when they mutually decided to end their relationship, it was amicable.

I went on two or three dates with a young lady who admitted that she was a "bedside Baptist." What she meant was that she worshiped God while lying in bed instead of going to church (Heb 10:25). I still enjoyed spending time with her, but we both knew that our relationship had no real future. Today we are still friends and respect one another. Nothing physical ever happened between us and we were both okay with that.

I dated two other young ladies (at different times); one was divorced and the other was a widow, and both indicated that they had been called into the ministry. I enjoyed spending time with both of them, as we obviously had a great deal in common. We talked extensively about our relationships with the Lord and our goals in life. Yet, it became apparent that they were more concerned with their role as ministers of the Gospel than dating or marriage, and I was fine with that. I am friends with both young ladies now, and I still respect them as Christians and women of God.

In Exodus 33:7-11, Moses set an example for intimacy with God because he was willing to be subjected to God. As a Christian, you must be willing to endure discomfort and possibly pain while you attempt to live the Christian life on this side of death (Eph 6:12). Weeping may endure for a night, but joy cometh in the morning, (Ps 30:5), even when others criticize us and we feel alone (I King 19:3-4, Ps 31:9-12). Sometimes within our social networks and within our community, we are lonely because we are isolated by information, isolated by obedience (Jeremiah 1:19;16:1,2), or isolated by demands. However, it is our responsibility to set an example for others because people believe what they see. Your behavior during the dating process must demonstrate that you love God and that you are serious about your Christian walk. Moses demonstrated this truth. People watched him as he spent time with God by separating himself and seeking God with all his heart (Exodus 33:7), knowing he was being watched by the people (33:8). He listened to God's voice and entered into covenant partnership with him (33:10, 11).

For example, if, during the dating process, we make it clear that we want to be equally yoked with a person we are dating exclusively and will not settle for anything less, this lifestyle makes us unique and separates us from others. Some spiritual lessons can only be learned in the crucible of profound loneliness. Jesus wanted to keep his closest companions with him during what he anticipated would be an enormous trial. No one wants to be alone at a time like that (Matt 26:36-46); However, Jesus did endure it alone, but at the same time he was not really alone because God was with him and is always with us (Ps 3:3-8; 139:7-8).

Slippery when Wet

Someone once said that he who does not want to fall down should not walk on slippery surfaces.

Now pay attention, young men and women, as I don't want you to miss this. Sometimes, just because you are equally yoked does not mean that you are equally compatible. Think of it this way. You might have a shiny, brand new Cadillac, and you might be cruising down the highway and traveling a little faster, in the rain, than you should. You're not worried, though, because after all, you're driving a Cadillac, which is considered a top of the line luxury car equipped with some of the best tires and suspension system on the market. Yet, you have forgotten that when oil and water mix, it does not matter what kind of car you're driving or what type of tire is on the car.

Any vehicle is capable of sliding and not stopping under the right conditions. And guess what? You could crash or, at the very least, run off the road. The tires on your car are not compatible with the pavement because of the weather conditions. There are no potholes in the street, and the tires have excellent tread, but the rain and oil that represent each of your personalities can make traveling very hazardous, particularly when you are going too fast. You can't assume that just because the person you are seeing was raised in the church that the church was raised in them.

What Do You Like Now?

Do you enjoy the same things now that you enjoyed ten or twenty years ago, apart from church? Do you participate in the same activities? Watch the same programs? Hang around the same friends? Vacation in the same places? Attend the same church? Maybe you do but probably not, because we evolve as people and our bodies change. I can't run up and down a basketball court like I could ten or fifteen years ago; I don't watch programs on TV in the same manner that I did in the seventies, eighties, or nineties; and I certainly don't eat as much as I did in the past .

As a result, you need to take a hard and honest look at what you enjoy, how you like to spend your time, what your interests are, and what your dreams, aspirations, and fears are *now*. For example, I owned a dog in the past and I still like dogs. I also enjoyed bowling and being a member of a bowling league. But do I want to own a dog now? Do I want to be committed to a bowling team now? No! Making a commitment to take care of an animal, to bowl on a regular basis, or to participate in a ballroom dancing class simply does not interest me *now*. Determining what you like now is essential, and until you do, you are destined to have difficulty dating and developing a relationship with a member of the opposite sex.

My wife, Kattie, was a widow when we started dating, and initially we hung out as friends. We learned that we were both Cleveland Browns fans (don't hold it against us), Piston fans, and sports fans in general. In addition, I was a widower. We practiced the same faith, and attending church and serving God was a key value we both shared. As we were both parents and homebodies," i.e., the "street life" was not appealing to us, we also shared a certain selflessness that permeated our relationship. We both had children, and although mine were much older than hers, it still became apparent that rearing and being there for our children was and still is important to us. We were developing a friendship.

However, sometimes society makes it difficult for singles to have friends. Our friends mean well, but sometimes they are always trying to fix us up and assume that the person you are dating is "the one." Why couldn't we just be friends? My wife was not looking for a husband, and I was not looking for a wife. We were looking for *companionship.* My challenge was intellectual compatibility and to resist the urge to "dumb down" to date. I tried to explain to a few of the women that I dated that just because I had an advanced degree that did not mean I was smart. Common sense is not always common, and I could sometimes say and do some dumb stuff. However, whenever there was a disagreement or a problem to resolve, my education always seemed to enter the discussion. I would hear comments like "You have the PhD, why can't you figure it out?" or "I will let you figure it out because you have a Ph.D" or "I guess I am stupid because I don't have a doctorate like you do." I began to develop a complex about my education. I knew that if I were to marry again that I needed a woman who was very secure with who she was and not intimidated by my credentials.

Lorraine, my first wife who left me a widower, had only a high school education, but she was very, very smart. In many ways she was smarter than I. She was a financial wizard, an exceptional student in a paralegal program, and would probably have earned a law degree if the Lord had not taken her home. She loved to read, and was a relentless researcher and an excellent writer. Kattie is without a doubt the smartest person I know (much smarter than I), and she is also a very talented administrator, writer, and accountant who thinks outside the box in astonishing ways. Yet, having a degree was never a prerequisite before I started dating Lorraine or Kattie. I did not learn that Kattie even had a degree until months after we started seeing each other. In-depth conversations about life, love, God, our goals in life, values, sex, and child rearing revealed that we were compatible and that she was very secure and comfortable with who she was. We connected mentally, emotionally, spiritually, and with God's help we connected in the sexual arena. (Thank you Jesus!)

Dating Issues: Millennials, Gen Xs, and Baby Boomers

Who are these generations, you may ask? The answer is as easy as X, Y, and Z. In broad (completely unfair) terms, Generation X (born between 1966 and 1976) is commonly characterized by apathy, cynicism, and general disengagement from social issues; Generation Y (born between 1977 and 1994) oozes technological sophistication, an almost slavish addiction to fads, and (until recently) easy access to credit. If there's one thing that characterizes baby boomers — the generation born between 1946 and 1964 — it's the belief that they can have it all. Single boomers can date freely amongst the younger generations, regardless of the pop-cultural disconnect that may exist between them. And Generation Z? Well, we'll have to wait to see how that group turns out; you shouldn't really think about dating them yet, since the oldest members are barely young adults.

Okay, of course, there are many exceptions. Some Gen-Xers are married, earnest, and optimistic, and it's statistically likely that at least some Gen-Yers, also known as millenials, have never used Twitter or listened to 50 Cent. I assume they are prowling the internet and hiding the fact they are bald, forty-seven-year-old men.

Regardless of generalities people might make about any of these age groups, when it comes to love, pretty much everyone is still looking for exactly the same thing. Deep down, some boomers and a significant number of people in general are still just teenagers at heart. I know that when I first started dating, my daughter, who was living with me at the time, commented that I was acting like a teenager who had just been introduced to dating. She pointed out that when she observed me talking on the phone in my bedroom late at night, with the lights off and using a very low, hushed tone, she knew I was dating because that's what she used to do. We want love, romance, time, attention, and affection. That never changes. Consequently, regardless of which generation a person has been born into, the needs of that person in the context of dating are consistent with the needs of those born in other generations.

Most boomers will deny it, but dating someone a generation (or more) younger is usually a transparent gambit to recapture some lost sense of youth. A person shouldn't choose a younger partner just to roll back the clock. If a couple is going to develop a healthy, long-term relationship, they need to consider the love they share for each other, their commonality of interests, their life goals, and their ability to communicate. Of course, a ten-year age difference is much more appropriate than a twenty-year difference when you consider the health and energy of your partner in the years to come.

Here are a few suggestions for uncovering what you like now:

- Make sure that you know your own doctrine (I Tim 3:15), that is, what is being taught at your church. In my estimation, it is almost impossible to understand if you are equally yoked if you don't know your own doctrine (Ephesians 4:14) and what you really believe. I am not suggesting that you prepare yourself to debate someone you are dating about your faith. Discussion and dialogue are always appropriate, as the Lord, with the help of the Holy Ghost, may guide you to witness to this person and possibly lead them to Christ. But if you don't know your own doctrine, you will have a problem in this area.
- Make every effort to join the person you are dating in private and public worship; attend church, worship, pray, and read the Word with them. Even if you say to yourself, "Well, we are just kicking it. I don't intend to marry them," you should still worship with them if possible. This is so important because if you do encounter someone whose worship experience is different from what you are accustomed to, you will be more

comfortable participating in that worship experience with a person you really like even if your approach to worship may be different. Be willing to step outside your comfort zone. But knowing your own doctrine first is crucial.

- It is imperative that you know yourself well enough and be secure enough with yourself to engage a person in an honest dialogue about faith, worship, doctrine, the bible and prayer.
- If you were born in different generations, make a concerted effort to learn the tendencies and values of individuals born within the other person's generation.
- Be willing to take a personality inventory with the help of your primary care physician or a trained counselor. You might be surprised at what you might find out about yourself. You must be willing to honestly examine yourself.
- If you are a homebody and consider yourself boring, be willing to step out of your comfort zone and explore areas you never thought you might like.
- Ladies, trust me, if you take it upon yourself to learn all you can about football or basketball, most of the guys you date will be blown away.
- Guys, get comfortable with all kinds of shopping (furniture, clothes), even if you don't buy anything. Find out what adventurous women like. Some like to try different things. Find out what those are and learn to enjoy them.
- Don't hesitate or be afraid to have very candid conversations with the person you are seeing about life, God, goals, hobbies, sex, church, entertainment, finance, debt, and anything else that is important to you.

Chapter IV

S-L-O-W Down

O nce you know who you are and have some understanding of how secure you are as a man or women, you need to S-L-O-W down: **S**ee what you need to see; **L**isten to what you don't want to hear; **O**bserve circumstances, environments, and situations; **W**ait before making any decisions. You need to slow down. When you don't take the time required to uncover as much information as you possibly can about a person you are dating, the relationship is destined to crash.

See What You Need to See: Often you see what you want to see but not what you need to see. You are so convinced that this person is "the one" that you simply dismiss or ignore indicators that a few issues exist that could be deal-breakers. I am not talking about the fact that the person eats with their mouth open, interrupts you when you're talking, or simply tends to think that he or she is always right when discussing an issue. You can work through these things. However, you should know what your deal-breakers are. One example might be if your dating partner too often displays a tendency to place a higher value on his or her family relationships than devoting time to developing a relationship with you.

Listen to What You Don't Want to Hear: I was dating a young lady and I noticed right away that, for no reason, she frequently engaged in arguments with people she did not even know—vendors, cashiers, and salespeople, for example. At first I labeled her behavior as feistiness. Oh, she just has a lot of "spunk." Yet after a while, that "spunk" turned into "funk" and spilled over into several verbal exchanges we had. I had to listen. This young lady's challenge in problem solving was something I had not experienced before in a relationship. Consequently, when I began to hear these hostile verbal exchanges, I was stunned, thought they might go away, and convinced myself that all of her positive attributes outweighed this character flaw. I was wrong.

<u>Observe Circumstances, Environments, and Situations:</u> It has been my experience that one method for getting to know a person you are dating is to travel with them. It does not mean that you need to sleep in the same hotel room or practically live with the person. It just means planning a series of short, one-day excursions that involve devoting some quality time to this person. As you plan the trip, you can observe his or her process for decision-making, how the person manages the resources for the trip, how they prepare, and how they deal with conflict or unexpected problems you encounter. You can learn a lot about a person by just watching and listening.

<u>Wait before Making Any Decisions:</u> When my children have sought my advice (and even when they haven't), I have consistently told them that if they are meant to be with a person they are dating, then there is no need to rush. I was counseling a couple who had been married less than a year, and who had met online and married within six months of meeting. Their problems stemmed from the simple fact that they really did not know each other at all and were just in too much of a hurry.

I think there are at least four stages of dating that Kattie and I and even Lorraine and I experienced. The first stage is uncertainty. When you meet someone you are thinking about dating, it is normal to be uncertain of whom you are dealing with. Kattie was uncertain of whether she should go out with me, and Lorraine was very hesitant as well. There is no need to rush. Even after two people begin to date, some uncertainty still exists before you move to the level of exclusivity or dating only one person. One of the first questions that probably has crossed your mind is how long you should date a person before you move to the exclusive stage. There is no set time; it varies from relationship to relationship, and there are no guarantees that a relationship will be successful regardless of how long you wait. Some marriages have lasted for years after the man and woman dated only a few months, but those are the exceptions. I have lived and advised my children to live by the "think six months" rule, meaning don't even think seriously about dating a person exclusively until after at least six months. Kattie and I dated for two months before I even kissed her. I dated one Christian young lady for at least six months and we never kissed. Why? Because that next stage (possible intimacy) should not occur if you have not reached exclusivity.

Intimacy, which can range from holding hands to warm embraces to a foot massage, can be defined in a variety of ways. You need to talk about what it means to each of you and to know each other's danger zones. The next stage is engagement and then, of course, marriage. However, I also don't think engagement should even be discussed until after at least a year and, in some cases, engagements should be extended. I was talking with a friend who got engaged recently and was experiencing some uncertainty because of a few problems that had surfaced in the relationship. I encouraged her to consider extending the engagement. Financial considerations aside, sometimes, depending on how serious the issues are, some marriages should be postponed for obvious reasons.

Patience: Don't Get a Speeding Ticket

Have you ever received a speeding ticket? Don't lie. Of course, you have (or at least a warning). If you haven't received either or a have not been cited for some type of moving violation, I am sure that (unless you started driving yesterday) you caught yourself exceeding the speed limit and slowed down because you either saw a police car or your conscience told you to do so. But for those of you who have, it has been my experience that something strange happens after you are cited. It seems like from that point on for at least the next fifty miles and sometimes for the next week or month, you almost feel like an imaginary highway patrolman is still watching you, even though he or she is no longer on the scene. You automatically slow down and it seems like everybody else is speeding. The only reason you are motivated to slow down is that the thought of a fine (money), elevated insurance rates (more money), points on your driving record (even more money), and possible embarrassment. There is a penalty to pay when we travel too fast, and it is the same with relationships.

Sometimes you are moving too fast in a relationship but are oblivious to your speed because you are either enjoying the ride so much or are simply accustomed to traveling fast. You don't even notice how fast you are going! You don't begin to slow down until the wrong relationship—and issues that surface in the relationship—require you to pay a hefty price emotionally, financially, or professionally. I made the mistake of allowing that infatuation stage to cause me to waste money, time, and resources. In one situation, I put my reputation on the line because I *thought* I knew the young lady I had been seeing.

Sometimes the positive aspects of your personality can create a problem for you as you deal with others because some people will tend to see your kindness as a sign of weakness. You must *slow down* and take the time to find out with whom you are really dealing. I like to think of relationships in the context of the movie *Titanic*. In the film, the captain had a conversation with one of the crew members about how fog and the increased speed of the ship might make it difficult to spot an iceberg. Well, we know what happened; by the time the iceberg was spotted, it was too late and the ship crashed. Research has shown that you can only see ten percent of an iceberg above the waterline. Above a person's "waterline" you *see* attire and various aspects of the anatomy, and in conversations you may learn about all kinds of *superficial* things such as how they feel about the weather, animals, or your cologne. But until you lower the waterline and learn more about a person's values, attitudes, beliefs, and patterns of thinking, you won't really know that person. You can't lower the waterline when you are moving too fast. As a result, some relationships crash (and sink!) in the same way that the *Titanic* did. We simply have a tendency to move too fast, and we need to slow down.

My wife Kattie and I were discussing some of the concepts I cover in this book, and she asked me a question I'd never been asked before. She said, "Did you ever enjoy being single? Did you ever enjoy not being accountable to anyone? Being able to come and go as you pleased? Not being responsible for anyone but yourself?"

I thought about what she had asked me for a few minutes before I responded. Then I replied that having that kind of flexibility, a lack of accountability to anyone or anything, had been very convenient and initially very enjoyable. I said that I had always enjoyed traveling, and so driving to another city sometimes on the spur-of-the-moment was fun and exciting. However, I added that my problems began after I arrived at my destination and completed whatever activity I had traveled to participate in (a conference, class reunion, vacation etc.) or at times during the activity. If I was having fun, I always had a strong desire to share the experience with a female companion. If I was not having a good time, I felt even worse. I am reminded of the old saying that "nobody likes to drink alone" because you tend to get even more depressed. Although I don't drink, the analogy strongly suggests that you tend to enjoy life in general a little more in the company of another person. Therefore, it is even more crucial that you really invest the time you need to find the right person to with whom spend quality time.

Another way to explain it is through the concept of entropy, the second law of thermodynamics. It means deterioration when something or someone is isolated. That is one reason why we, as mere mortals, have such a strong need and desire for companionship. In the movie *The Intern*, Robert DeNiro played a retired executive who was a widower. He said that although he enjoyed traveling, when he reached his destination, he realized that he did not have anywhere to be. That is exactly how I felt at times.

Everybody is different, and if you have never experienced these feelings, that's understandable. In addition, I am sure that a significant number of people in general—and men in particular—enjoy being single and would not change anything. That's fine, but I am not talking to those people. I am talking to the person who may have felt the way I did. I suspect if any of you ever went out on a date with the wrong person, if you are honest with yourself, you felt even lonelier. You might even have wished that you had gone alone. That's why it is important that you take your time. S-L-O-W down! Try not to be in a rush. You might hate to see the weekends come, but you have to be patient. You might hate it when married couples invite you over for dinner—and you imagine they are feeling sorry for you— but you must be patient. You might hate it if, when you are out with a female friend, your married friends see you and practically start making your wedding plans.

You have to remind yourself that the person who becomes your companion is someone you will be spending vacations, weekend excursions, and quality time with, hopefully for the balance of your life. Because many of us desire companionship so much, feelings of impatience can be very difficult to handle. One of the primary reasons we are so impatient is that patience is not, never has been and never will be a virtue that many of us have in abundance. Of course, some of you are more patient than others, but most of us are primarily egocentric and have been socialized to live in a "right now" culture. And those who are dating or engaged are no different.

Part of the problem is that all of you hate this nine-letter word called "rejection," and when you are dating, it is impossible not to experience the feelings that result from being rejected. Feelings of confusion, frustration, anger, doubt, anxiety, and sadness abound when one experiences the R-word, and when we do, we want to try to avoid these feelings as much as possible.

Remember that rainy, cloudy evening that I reflected on at the beginning of Chapter I? Another emotion or feeling that you might experience (but would rather not acknowledge) when rejection occurs is *fear.* Fear that you will not find anyone, that you might be destined to remain alone. Many of you have heard one acronym for FEAR: False Evidence Appearing Real. However, there is another acronym that says we should Forget Everything and Run! Yet, we must be careful to avoid running into the arms of the wrong person or lay our head in the lap of the wrong woman! Samson learned that the hard way (Judges 16:19).

Samson knew his strength was in his hair and if he revealed that information to anyone, it could be used against him. What you must understand about Samson is that before he met Delilah, he told his parents he wanted to take a wife from the Philistines (Judges 14:3). His parents warned against this, but he did so anyway, which is similar to what happens when people you love and trust advise you to stay away from certain people you are thinking about dating and you ignore their advice. Or you don't even seek the advice of people you trust, even though—like your children—they might be the people who know you best. To make matters worse, Samson ignored the very God who had given him the gift of strength and became involved with a harlot. Consequently, by the time Delilah appeared on the scene, Sampson had become comfortable with being led by the flesh and not by the Spirit of God. We walk by faith and not by sight (II Cor 5:7).

On the other hand, you may wonder why it needs to take so long. As I mentioned in Chapter I, being friends with a woman was something I did not know how to do. Therefore, when I started dating after becoming a widower, I found myself evaluating each woman in the context of whether she could possibly become a lifelong partner. I think that because celibacy was very important to me, I knew that if I did not live in a holy way, God would not be pleased with me and would hold me accountable if I lived a life that would not be pleasing to him. (Gal 6:7-8)). I believe that a Christian man who genuinely wants to live for the Lord will allow the Holy Spirit to help him to hold himself to a higher standard of living.

I think that young ladies should be very suspicious of engagements that last for more years than a reasonable person would expect. Although every engagement is different, some are simply too long. There needs to be a clear understanding of what both of you would like to see happen during this period and how long it will that take for that to happen. For example, do both individuals think extensive marital counseling is needed? Can you set a date, or at least a tentative date that you could change before making an official announcement? How do both of you feel about sex prior to marriage? If marriage is what you are working toward, these seem like reasonable questions.

A significant number of men—even some Christian men, unless they are embracing celibacy—will gladly "have their cake and eat it too." You probably will not respect a woman as much if she does not respect her own body. Ladies, do not let the fear of losing that man motivate you to continue allowing him to use you. Some men (and women) really don't want to get married and are not ready to commit, to make a marriage work.

Let me explain. A person may want a companion, a role model for their child or children, someone to share expenses with, or may simply want to quit being, "single and sinning," (sexually) but they are not really prepared or willing to put in the hard work it takes to make a marriage work. There is a big difference. The person God has for you—who is willing and able, with the help of God, to live a supernatural-selfless life with you—might be waiting until you rid yourself of the man who won't commit to you. If you are good enough for him to sleep with, you are good enough for him to marry. I would venture to say that the man had a very good idea of whether you could be "the one" before he slept with you.

Dating is not an exact science because men and women are different. Achieving goals is always very important to most men. It is a way for a man to demonstrate competence and feel worthwhile and secure. To use clothes shopping as an example, most men go into a store, make the purchase, and leave. As we all know, the shopping experience for most women is a little different. It's usually much longer, involves the touching and stroking of the various garments, and is a more intimate experience. Between my mid-twenties and my mid-forties, I wanted to scream every time I realized I had allowed myself to end up at the Mall with my wife and a checkbook. I could never figure out how it happened and would invariable wonder how I'd gotten myself into it. Even as I surveyed my surroundings, I could not find any support from other men because most of them were either sitting down from exhaustion or looking equally helpless or trapped. However, as I allowed the wisdom of God to speak to me, I learned to view the shopping experience from my wife's perspective. Although I still value getting in and out of stores quickly, if I am with my wife, I genuinely enjoy the experience because I love and enjoy being with her and seeing her happy. Besides it's good exercise.

If a man can work toward displaying such a selfless attitude, it minimizes the natural tendency most man have to be autonomous, which is a symbol of efficiency, power, and competence. Unfortunately we men tend to get so wrapped up in ourselves and doing our own thing that we forget God has said that it is not good for man to be alone (Genesis 2:18) and that two are better than one (Ecclesiastes 4:10-11). If you are a man and you recognize that you need help, it is a sign of wisdom (Proverbs 1:7), and most of you will seek out someone you respect because of your tendency as a man to be efficient and competent, and to do things quickly.

Most men either don't need much time or simply won't take much time to decide if a woman is "the one." I am not saying that a one-, two-, or even three-year engagement is inappropriate. I am suggesting that a significant number of men—particularly Christian men—who are genuinely interested in marriage don't need six months or a year before deciding to date a woman exclusively and eventually marry. For some men, the older and more experienced you are, the wiser you are in terms of making these types of decisions. (See Chapter I: Self-awareness). One size does not fit all. And of course, if you have no desire to serve the Lord and consequently are not being guided by the Holy Spirit, you are certainly more inclined to allow your nature (and I am not talking about mother nature) to guide your decision-making process. But because of a significant number of conversations I have had with men, and from my own personal experience, coupled with the advent of online dating, I find that men seem to make these decisions much sooner.

At the risk of sounding repetitious, knowing yourself well enough to know what you want in a relationship is crucial. If you are looking for a husband, tell him. If you are looking for a wife, tell her. If you would prefer not to date just to be dating, tell the other person. If you feel like you are not interested in the "friends with benefits" mindset, explain that as well. It is crucial that we know whether we are single and satisfied, single and seeking, or single and sinning. One characteristic of being single and satisfied is that we might feel that we have a special "call" to singleness. This call might have you feeling natural and peaceful to be free of any spousal encumbrances. I will discuss this more in Chapter VIII. You must seek God's guidance, but it is important not to idealize marriage too much. God did not create you to be desperate. Desperation stems from feelings of hopelessness that can cause you to behave irrationally, resulting in confusion. Let everything be done decently and in order (I Cor 14:40) because God is not the author of confusion (I Cor 14:33). If you are single and seeking, then you are actively seeking a partner, and if you are single and sinning, then Satan, your flesh, and the world have convinced you to ignore what God has said in his Word about our bodies (I Cor 6:19) and the consequences of our behavior (Gal 6:7 Roman 6:23). Here are a few suggestions:

- Be willing to discuss intimacy, what it means to you, and how you think it should be approached.
- Be willing to discuss male and female relationships in general.
- Whatever your "bedrock" attitudes are, stick to them. A man or woman will respect you for that.

Money

Now men and ladies, be *very* suspicious if the issue of money surfaces in terms of someone wanting to spend yours. Borrow, loan, hold or whatever they want to call, it still means . . . spend your money! A very good friend of mine gave money to a young lady he had known less than a week, a female friend "loaned" money to a person she had met online and was never repaid, and I (yes, yours truly) gave a significant amount of money to a woman I had met online. Now the question is why? Why would any of these very intelligent, emotionally stable, people of moderate means give money away? Particularly someone as cheap as me? My brother once said I was so cheap that I could squeeze the buffalo off a nickel. Well, I am not that cheap, but I don't know why I was so gullible. Yet, I can speculate. I think all of us were vulnerable, somewhat naïve, and financially able to do it, but most importantly, we were convinced that we knew what we were doing. I mean all of us had been married before, had grown children, and had been accustomed to making difficult decisions, right? Why wouldn't we know what we were doing? But that's the "angle" or argument of the enemy Satan. He knows your weaknesses and knows your personalities. He is very shrewd, cunning, and full of tricks (Genesis 3:5, Ephesians 4:14). He appeals to your flesh and will suggests to you, like he suggested to Eve, that you don't need God to make decisions in your lives. You can do it on your own. Unscrupulous people prey on those who are ripe for the picking. He catches you when you are weak and most vulnerable.

Children

I am a grandfather, great-grandfather and stepfather. Both of my stepchildren are younger than my eldest granddaughter, I have six grandchildren and two great-grandchildren, and I have a host of nieces and nephews. As a result, children, both biological and non-biological, have been a part of my life for over four decades. I am a veteran at blending families, but not an expert. However, when I became a widower, the first criteria I had for dating were that the woman not be of childbearing age and any children she had needed to be at least young adults.

The problem was that I had not consulted the Lord about my criteria. As I began walking closer with him, I concluded that God knew my heart and I grew to understand and accept the fact that the Lord's will for my life was much more important than my own agenda. If it was not in his will for me to remarry, I was at peace with that. Conversely, if it was in his will for me to remarry, I had to trust that he would lead me to the women he wanted me to have. I needed to believe that, because he had created me and knew me better than I knew myself (Psalms 139), he would make available to me the type of woman I needed. But equally important was that I needed to process my feelings about children. Did I want to be a stepfather again? As I discussed in Chapter I, self-awareness is crucial before a person who is single begins this journey. I decided, with the help of the Lord and advice from a Christian young lady I had met during my journey, that a woman and her children could still benefit from my life experiences, and if the Lord wanted me to be a role model for another generation of children, I was at peace with that as well. I was just elated that the Lord and I were on the same page regarding toddlers not being in my future!

Sharing your thoughts about children with a person you are dating exclusively is very important. Even if you don't marry the person, mothers and fathers need to be cautious and extremely careful when considering the possibility of introducing their children to someone they are dating. The following are just a sample of the kinds of questions they need to ask.

- How were they reared?
- Was the father authoritative, dogmatic, kind, gentle, mean?
- Were both parents in the home?
- What was their relationship like?
- How does the person feel about children?
- How do they feel about being around *your* children?
- What values, attitudes, and beliefs were they reared to embrace?
- Does anyone in the family have alcohol or drug problems?
- Has the person had any children out of wedlock?

If you are dating someone who professes to love the Lord, it is essential that you have a candid conversation about child-rearing philosophies. You might want to share with the person that research has shown that the primary cause for children being in foster homes is not divorce, financial destitution, or death of their parents, but simply the disinterest of their parents. Therefore, one question you might need to ask yourself is whether this person would be interested in your child or children. Is disinterest or neglect a form of child abuse? Another topic that should be discussed is the role of the father and mother. Who should be the primary disciplinarian? Do you and the person you are dating agree that parents should bring up children in the "discipline and instruction of the Lord?" (Ephesians 6:4b). The conversation could also involve how each of you feels about the importance of trying to praise children more often, encourage them, and share God more intimately with them (Proverbs 17:6).

During one of my recent sermons, I also told the men it was imperative that they develop relationships with their daughters and nieces, if they have them. I said that unfortunately their daughters and nieces would, from time to time, encounter men who would not treat them with respect, and could have a very abusive attitude toward them. As a result, they might be the only men in their lives that these young ladies could turn to for comfort, advice, understanding, and direction. Ladies, do you feel that the man you are dating is able to model how a real man should treat a woman? It's something to think about.

Step parenting

My definition of a stepfather or stepmother differs from the traditional definition. Since I have functioned as a stepfather on one previous occasion and am currently a stepfather, I think that qualifies me to develop a definition that might work better for some people. I think a stepparent is a person who "steps into the gap" which was created when the biological parent was removed from a child's life, either voluntarily or involuntarily. The question you need to ask yourself is whether the person you're dating or considering dating is capable and willing to step into the gap. Also consider the following:

- Do they talk about children in a positive way?
- How do they treat their children if they have any?

- If they have nieces and nephews, do they have a relationship with them?
- Do they even like children?
- Do they seem to have a flexible personality?
- How selfless are they?
- Do they understand that adults make memories for children each and every time they interact with them?
- Do they understand that it will be their responsibility to earn the trust and respect of a child and not vice-versa?

I remember when Kattie and I first started dating. Her concern and the concern of her seventeen-year-old daughter was whether I would ever gain the approval of the baby boy, who was fifteen at the time. I wasn't concerned because I knew in my heart that I really cared, respected, and loved their mother, and that he would see that right away. In addition, I knew that I needed to be very patient with both of her children. I understood that they were still grieving for their biological father and that each was at a very critical stage in their life as young adult and teenager respectively. I also understood that relationships take time to develop, that you can't rush them, and he and his sister should be very protective of their mother. I also observed that the family was very close and that Kattie's siblings were very involved in the lives of her children. As a result, I was prepared for the siblings to talk with everybody they knew about me. I also learned that her eldest sibling had been a member of my church for several years, and I never knew that they were related. Thank God I had tried to live an upright holy life because if I had not, I am sure her sister would have known it.

During a recent conversation with a young man, he shared with me an experience he had with a young lady he was thinking about dating. They were in the preliminary stages and talking about a variety of things, including sports, the weather, and careers. However, during one of those conversations, the young lady began questioning him about his divorce and negative statements made in the divorce decree about his temperament, character, and how he interacted with his children. She had retrieved the records from the archives of the local family court. The conversation became very heated and at one point argumentative. Yet he indicated that it ended on a positive note after she explained why she had gotten the court records. In a previous marriage, her husband had pointed a weapon at her and threatened to shoot her. Consequently, she had been very cautious and skeptical about any man she dated.

I told this young man not to take her actions personally, and she should have been more patient and allowed the information about his divorce to surface naturally during conversations about his life. Her intent was understandable, but her method was inappropriate and probably indicative of a person who was still under construction. As a former EEO compliance officer, I have conducted at least a hundred investigations of Sexual Harassment Complaints and throughout my career I have facilitated anti-harassment training sessions for at least 15,000 individuals. My conclusion was that not all men are abusers of women, but most abusers are men

Trust . . . but Verify

It is amazing to me how adept people are at showing another person one the side of them that they want that person to see. I recall one situation at a church where a young man proposed to a young lady in front of the congregation where the young lady was a member. The young man had visited this church on several occasions while he was dating her, but he never married her. He displayed to the church and to the young lady that he was charming, bold, and engaging. However, in reality, he was untrustworthy, shallow, and deceptive. He only showed his former fiancée and the church the side of him that he wanted them to see. His heart was not in the right place.

This reminds me of a story about two brothers. One became a farmer and the other became a wealthy lawyer on Wall Street. The lawyer visited the farmer and said to him, "Look at me. I am a very successful lawyer on Wall Street. I have clients who are worth millions of dollars, and here you are still stuck on this farm. Tell me, what is the difference between you and me?" The farmer asked his wealthy brother to look at the wheat that was standing tall in the field and the wheat that was bent over. He said that the wheat standing tall was empty on the top, but the wheat that was bent over was full. He indicated that people who are standing tall are often empty, but the ones who are a bent over are full, which means that what matters is not in your head but in your heart. The young lady who received that marriage proposal at her church did not know the young man well enough to allow God to reveal to her the condition of his heart before she entrusted him with her own.

Normally the issues I cover in this section would not be addressed until after two people are considering engagement. However, the proliferation of online dating sites, scam artists, and dishonest practices throughout our society, and the fact that a significant number of people in our society subscribe to the eleventh commandment, "Thou shall not get caught," mean that the following areas need to be addressed as early in a relationship as possible.

Regardless of the lies we tell ourselves, love really is conditional. Love is conditioned on the truth, and an omission can constitute a lie. Reportedly, a former president's political stance toward the Soviet Union was "Trust . . . but verify." I think we should take this same position in dating, dating exclusively, and especially prior to engagement or marriage. As stewards of the resources that God has entrusted us with, it is our responsibility, not only to ourselves but to God as well, to be prudent in the use and handling of our resources, particularly money. Luke 16:1-8 talks about our use of money as a good test of the Lordship of Christ. We must use our resources wisely and handle money carefully and thoughtfully.

In addition, I think we must use one of the most precious resources we have as wisely as we can, and that is how we spend our time. We don't have as much of it as we think we do. Therefore, I am convinced that a verification search involving at least forty areas take place, but if time and finances constitute a problem, I believe that if any "red flags" exist, they will surface through verification of the following twenty:

- Birth records
- Bankruptcies
- Civil Court records and judgments
- County Criminal Records check
- Credit Bureau checks (all three companies)
- Divorce records
- Motor Vehicle records
- Employment verification
- Marriage Licenses
- Social Security Number
- Sexual Offender search
- Nationwide Criminal Record
- Federal Bankruptcy Lien System
- Google.com
- National death index
- Assumed names - County Clerk Registration
- State Department of Corrections online offender name search
- Voter Registration
- Tax lien system
- How to investigate.com

Please note that during my discussion earlier about the young man who acted angrily toward the young lady he was "thinking" about dating who pulled his divorce records has to be put in perspective. I am not suggesting that a background check be conducted on a person you just had a cup of coffee with and you're "considering" dating. The kind of background check mentioned earlier would be very appropriate after you have begun dating a person seriously.

Chapter V

Online and Long-Distance Dating

Sadly these days, there are many young ladies who are being coerced indirectly into bad situations because they met someone online. It is quite common for a young lady to be lured to a location to meet someone they don't know because they "fell in love" over the internet. Their initial relationship with this person was only by reading and a photo that may or may not be an accurate representation of the person. Both parties sit at their computer and read each other's words, but after a while the words take on life because behind the words is a real live person. Those words, particularly when addressed to someone who is vulnerable (Under Construction), grow into emotions and then turn into actions as both parties try to figure out a way to see each other. Those words take on life because both parties spend time abiding in the presence of someone they can not see. Unfortunately, those emotions will occasionally cloud or distort a person's judgment, particularly someone who is "under construction" or vulnerable. That is why it is important to abide with Jesus as much as possible (Romans 12:2; John 15:3-5), so when you do meet that person, the Lord can guide and minimize the possibility of your getting into a bad situation.

Attempting to meet someone online was for me initially fun and exciting. Communicating with a person who appeared to be attractive and with whom I had a lot in common was easy, safe, inexpensive, and required little time commitment. I could not have imagined a better way to enter the dating world. However, what I learned over a period of time was that dating online for me was like fool's gold. What I saw was not necessarily what I got. Meeting someone was not the problem. Developing "depth" in the relationship was, and that is what I was looking for. Please do not misunderstand me. I am not bashing online dating. I am sure a significant number of people have met their girlfriends or wives online and are living happily ever after. God bless them. But what you must keep in mind is that patience is not a common commodity. Whether you are single and satisfied, single and seeking, or single and sinning, it is easy to move from one category to the next if the person you view as "Mr. or Ms. Right" comes along, and Satan and the flesh do a good job of telling you that, since you like what you see, what are you waiting for? (Romans 7:15).

Ladies, unfortunately today it is necessary that you be even more cautious of men who use an online dating service. Again, don't misunderstand me. A lot of wonderful men are meeting women online. I know because at one time I was one of them, or at least I thought I was. But that could be where you might encounter problems. You need to ask yourself (and him) several questions. Are you aware of some of the pitfalls of dating online? Why is he online? Women generally outnumber men, so why is he using an online dating service? Is he just having fun?

I watched a movie entitled *How to Be Single,* and during one scene, a man and a woman who were dating had a conversation in which the man told the woman that he had been dating other people. She looked surprised. He said "Isn't that what people do who meet online?"

She retorted loudly, "*No,* you meet and date people online to find your soul mate!" Are the boundaries clearly established between you and this person? Are you just friends who are "kicking it?" (i.e. not serious). Apparently, one of the two characters in the movie I referred to was "kicking it" and the other one wasn't. Finally, are you secure enough with who you are to ask good, and sometimes hard, questions?

I think one of the primary reasons men and women are using an online dating service is because some are looking for a shortcut." One of my biggest fears and concerns when I was single was whether I would ever find someone I could trust. I simply did not want to go through the process of dating. In the words of a psychologist friend of mine, "kissing a lot of frogs" before finding a prince was not appealing to her. I thought that in the confines of my home and with my PC, I could avoid the expensive, time-consuming, sometimes painful, complex, emotionally draining, tedious, uncertain process of interacting with a member of the opposite sex.

There is no short cut. It's hard enough trying to develop depth in a relationship with a person of the opposite sex who lives down the street. Trying to develop this kind of depth with someone who lives in another city or state is twice as challenging, if that is what you are looking for. It always comes back to self-awareness. What do you want? The following suggestions might help you in the online dating world:

- Accept the fact that people lie. It's a fact of life, so don't be surprised when you find out that someone has not been honest with you, particularly someone you have met online. You must keep in mind that in the twenty-first century, some people will lie to your face, smile while they are doing it, and even stand up and defend the lie when they are caught out. Why wouldn't they lie online?
- Be very skeptical of all the photos people put online, especially headshots." (from the shoulders or waist up).
- Never give out personal information about yourself, and if you do decide to meet the person, women should make sure he comes to your city and not vice-versa.
- When the meeting does occur, make sure it is in a public place. In addition, I would suggest you have a friend close by.
- Conduct as much research as you possibly can about the person right away before you get "hooked" by their charm. If you can't find out anything about the person, stop right there.

(See the previous chapter.) That is not only a red flag, it could be downright dangerous!

- NEVER, NEVER, NEVER give money to anyone you have met online, no matter how sad their story is and even if you have it to give. You may not be the only one this person is asking for money.

Chapter VI

Flirting

Well, here we go . . . I am dating . . . now what???

To Flirt or Not to Flirt . . . That is the Question

Have you ever taken a car, particularly a new car, for a test-drive? Don't you love the smell of a new car? How about a car that has been well maintained and smells like new? Usually the ride is smooth, the brakes work well, you don't need to put any gas in the tank, and some dealers will allow you to keep it overnight. You can test-drive as many cars as you like, and you are not required to purchase any of them. But if you keep test-driving cars for fun and have no intention of purchasing one, after a while the dealer will probably get suspicious and question your creditability. Maybe you don't have the funds to make a commitment to purchase the automobile, or maybe you just like test-driving cars. I think that some forms of flirting are like test-driving a car. A person who enjoys driving a variety of cars, but has no intentions of purchasing one. The person who seems to show genuine interest but only wants to "make love without serious intentions" is similar to the test-driver.

What exactly is "flirting?" That is part of the problem because it means different things to different people. According to Webster's dictionary, to "flirt" means to "make love without serious intentions," to "play at love," and to move "back and forth." Although this is a very interesting definition, I doubt this is what a significant number of people *think* they are doing (playing at love?) or even thinking about when they flirt. I also realize that this dictionary definition may not be embraced by some people, and some of those same people will say that you can't define "flirting" in such a literal way. But we need to start somewhere.

The internet has various websites which maintain they can teach you to flirt effectively, and some of them are very interesting. Sites such as Quick Flirt, My Flirt, Flirt On, and Online Flirting are designed to assist anyone who wants to learn the art of flirting. In addition, two young ladies who were on the Tom Joyner Morning Show last year held a two-day retreat designed to show participants how to flirt. Apparently flirting has taken on a whole new meaning in the twenty-first century for men and women. Nonetheless, I also think that it has a *different* meaning for men than it does for women. As a result, you must be very careful about the messages you send when you set out to flirt.

Flirting with someone you know very well, especially if you have had a flirtatious relationship with them for an extended period of time and the flirtation is mutual, may be harmless. Both parties are mature, understand the boundaries, and have enough respect for each other to not cross the line. Yet even this kind of relationship has the potential to become a problem because what may seem harmless today may be viewed a little differently tomorrow, depending on what a person is going through. We see it all the time on television and in the real world. A person may start having marital or relationship problems, and because a person has been flirting with them on a regular basis, they might mistakenly think that this person is seriously attracted to them. As a result, the myth of "the grass is always greener" comes into play. The grass is always greener on the other side until you get over there, start walking on it, and realize it has to be watered, fertilized and mowed. Then you find out that grub mites (little parasites that destroy lawns)" have eaten away at the roots of the grass, and although the grass feels soft and looks good, the roots are eroded. The entire lawn then has to be replaced, which means, in the world of relationships, that the person is shallow, has no substance, and will continue to project a false image of himself or herself. ("Wow, that grass is so soft!"). After a while, the other person in the relationship wises up and gets out. Like the songwriter says, the love you saw in that person was just a mirage. That's what happens when one "plays at love" or "makes love without serious intentions" with someone who may in fact be looking for love. Nobody wants someone who plays with his or her emotions.

Kattie and I have talked about how I looked at her after our spouses had passed. She always said before we started dating, that I looked at her like I could "sop her up with a biscuit." But even she had to admit that, although I smiled at her, my eyes never roamed over her body,

I never winked at her, I always kept my distance, and I never made suggestive gestures with my mouth, hands, or eyes. She knew I liked talking with her and that I *probably* liked her, but she was not a hundred perfect sure. I smile a lot, I tend to make friends easily, and I am a good listener (although Kattie reminds me I am still a work in progress).

When I was dating, this type of personality served me well, but at times it was a problem. Learning to flirt was not something I had to learn how to do because some women I met thought that I was "always flirting" when I was simply being nice. When I was on the Tom Joyner Cruise 2009, I attended a networking session for businessmen and women to connect with one other, exchange business cards, and talk about the products we were selling. I could not convince Cybil, the TJMS moderator, that I was really there to network and not "hit on" the ladies." She thought I was only there to flirt when I was just being nice! It was not my fault that that I was the only male at the session. It's important to know who you are. You may not need to learn how to flirt.

Winking or smiling at a person, establishing eye contact, and indicating by your facial expression that you are interested are one thing. However, "elevator eyes," constantly commenting on a woman's anatomy, or making suggestive remarks to a woman ("Hey, when are you going to let me take you away for a weekend?") could move from flirtatious behavior to "I am seriously interested in *you* behavior."

It is crucial that you:

- Understand the boundaries of the relationship in general and what flirting means to both parties. It's okay to have fun with members of the opposite sex. However, does it always need to be of a flirtatious nature? Can't you joke about others things?
- Make sure that a person's kind, outgoing, fun-loving personality is not just a cover for someone who likes to flirt.
- Understand that everyone who smiles at you is not flirting.
- Don't convince yourself that eye contact has a "come hither" message. Giving eye contact while communicating with someone is demonstrating interest and respect. At the same time, staring into someone's eyes without a break could be construed as flirting.
- Beware of full-body embraces. This is particularly true for those of us in the church. You know what a brotherly or sisterly hug is. It is one you would give a sibling or Mother Anderson.
- Learn how to give a compliment. Saying "You look nice" is appropriate. "You look hot" is not appropriate because it has sexual connotations.

Dating in the Church

Can individuals who are members of the same church date each other? Are there similarities between dating members of your church and dating coworkers in the workplace? I think the answer to both questions is yes. Research has shown that fifty percent of the people who get married met their spouses at work. God has blessed thousands of individuals who met their spouses in church to marry and have spirit-filled lives. It happens all the time. However, the question is not whether a person should date a member of their church, but rather *how* the dating should unfold. That's where similarities to dating in the workplace exist. During my tenure as an EEO (Equal Employment Opportunity) executive, I investigated numerous allegations of sexual harassment, and I conducted hundreds of sexual harassment training sessions. In these sessions, I always indicated to faculty and staff that dating in the workplace was legal, permissible, and perfectly okay, but *risky*. Consequently, a tremendous amount of discretion was crucial because dating in the church is also *risky*. Dating multiple individuals in the church or in the workplace could be very problematic because one could be viewed as a person who preys on single women. (Certain women could wind up with a similar reputation.) Through *prayer* the Holy Spirit will guide you and help you recognize when the person arrives whom God he has selected for you, so that his will can be done, not yours (Philippians 2:13).

I know a young man who dated a young lady who was a member of his church. Yet when the relationship ended, hardly anybody at his church knew he and the young lady had been dating. It required discipline, effort, selflessness, and a spirit of humility, not only for them to use discretion while they were dating but also to end the relationship amicably. That way it was much easier for him to remain her brother in Christ and for her to remain his sister in Christ. It is never easy, but with God's help, it is possible.

However, he did make one mistake. If you recall I indicated that my first date with Kattie was during breakfast, which is the most appropriate way to meet with a young lady for the first time. Lunch would have worked just as well, but not dinner. Breakfast and lunch tend to be more informal and much less romantic than a dinner date. Much of the time dinner tends to be more intimate and could conceivably send a different message about one's intentions. Kattie and I had been seeing each other for a while before we had our first dinner date. I would suggest that until two people feel that the relationship has a very good chance of developing into something more than a passing friendship, one should be very cautious of the dinner date. Of course, if both parties are clear that the relationship is a mutual friendship, then that's a different story. No foul, no harm.

A Case Study (Carol and Arthur)

Arthur was sitting at his desk at work sifting through papers when his cell phone began to vibrate. When he saw the number on his caller ID, he did not recognize it, but he decided to answer the call. When he heard the voice of the caller, his heart sank as he recognized the voice as Carol's, and she was not someone he wanted to talk to. She said she was calling to apologize for the "problem" she had created with his car. She had taken his car without his permission, gotten into an accident, and damaged it beyond repair. In others words, "totaled" it.

She said that she did it because, as she knew he had another car and as he had loaned it to her previously, she did not think it would be a problem. Arthur thought he had lost the key to that car and assumed that someone had found the keys lying next to it, gone for a joy ride, and totaled it. He was stunned to learn that Carol, a former girlfriend, had taken his car without his permission. Arthur was hurt and shocked by such blatant disregard for his property, particularly when he had been so generous to her. He realized that he did not really know Carol at all.

Arthur's biggest concern was that he questioned his judgment and wondered if he should be dating anyone. He was so angry with Carol that he began feeling hatred toward her, and that frightened him because it was so uncharacteristic. He began to feel as if he had very little control over his life. Although they were members of the same church, Arthur had only been a member for a couple of years and Carol for four or five years. But more importantly, Arthur realized that for the good of the church (Romans 12:10) as well as his relationship with her and God, he needed to resolve the situation. He needed to allow the Holy Spirit to help him love her as a sister in Christ despite the pain she had inflicted on him. He knew that he needed to let it go and to take responsibility for his role in the situation. Thus, he forgave Carol and made peace with the matter. Arthur made, and is still making, a conscious effort to embrace the words that Jesus spoke on the cross when he had been betrayed, abandoned, and mistreated: "Father, forgive them for they know not what they do" (Luke 23:34). Carol and Arthur are not close friends, but they respect each other and greet each other warmly when they see each other in church.

As I have said previously, just because a person is in the church, it does not mean that the church is in him or her. Arthur made a lot of assumptions about Carol, and she probably made some assumptions about him since they attended and were active in the same church. (Carol sang in the choir and Arthur was a member of the usher board.) Some people have made peace with God and have therefore been freed from the penalty of sin (Romans 6:23). However, some of those same people still have not developed that peace of God that passeth all understanding (Phill 4:7), meaning that they are not as mature in their Christian walk as they could be.

A few suggestions:

- Be very prayerful, careful, and make sure you talk with your pastor about anyone you are thinking about dating in your church. Most pastors are a reservoir of information, and you would be surprised by what they know about church members that you don't know.

- Be discreet and make sure that the other person is also comfortable with being discreet. Making an announcement on a Sunday morning that you are dating would probably not be a good idea.

- Make sure that you are comfortable and mature enough to continue to worship with a person (or at least remain in the same building with the person) without feeling nervous, conflicted, or extremely uncomfortable if the relationship ends. A certain level of discomfort is to be expected initially but should dissipate after a while. If not, just remain patient and accept the fact that if you have been intimate with the person (heaven forbid!), you might need a little more time to get past the relationship.

- If conflict does occur, and it probably will, be a mature Christian and "take the high road," meaning you must be willing to apologize, even if you were not wrong. Offer to forgive the person if necessary and move on with your life. Is being right and winning in this spiritual tug of war worth sacrificing peace at your church and being at peace with yourself?

Chapter VII

Singles Ministries

After I began writing this book, I realized that although I felt that others could benefit from the insights I'd developed during the six or eight years I dated before I remarried, I thought that my readers could also benefit from what other Christian singles had to say about dating. So I contacted my younger brother, Bryan Hancock, who is single and who had a female friend in Columbus, Ohio named Rita, one of the leaders of a singles ministry at her church. I contacted Rita and, over the course of three months, she arranged for me to have a conversation with her individually and then to meet with the group collectively.

The first set of questions and answers are the results of questions Rita answered regarding dating. The second set is questions and answers from the group. Rita, age 57, is a business analyst and has never been married.

Dr. Sam: *Why are you still single?*

Rita: Interestingly enough, I never envisioned myself being unmarried and without children at this stage in my life. As a girl, I had my wedding songs and colors picked out. I planned to have three children, two boys first and then a girl. I even had the children named, including the first-born son as a junior. However, I truly believe God has preordained me to live my life as a single woman.

Although I always assumed that I would marry and start a family, I was actually extremely shy in my early years. I was also much smaller than my classmates and very youthful looking. So, I didn't have many boyfriends in high school.

Following high school, I enrolled at Ohio State University as a full-time student. My routine was to go to school and then to work. However, at the urging of my younger sister, we did go to the campus frat parties. Even though she was younger, she looked like the college student and I looked like the tag-along high school sister. Imagine which of us was asked to dance.

My career in banking began while attending college. A friend of mine, who was also a high school student yet way ahead of me socially, introduced me to Bryan Keith Hancock. We began dating, and I was taught to keep things under control. Life eventually took us in different directions. As my shyness began to dissipate, I became more of a leader, and my time became more focused on church and work. Family is also very important to me, and I now find myself leading my household with my mother as my priority. The point is that I am satisfied with where God has me and how he is using me.

Dr. Sam: *What are your thoughts about intimacy between two people who are not married but are dating exclusively?*

Rita: Mama said "No." I jokingly say that to my friends when conversations turn to related topics. Everyone laughs, but in all seriousness, I have committed myself to God, and I make every attempt to do the right thing in life. We all know what the Bible says, but it is a matter of what convicts you. You must consider whether "dating exclusively" guarantees marriage. Intimacy cannot be reversed, so consider how you would feel should you not marry your partner.

Dr. Sam: *What do you think are the challenges facing single men and women, particularly Christian men and women, in the dating world?*

Rita: Who is on the down low? (i.e trying to hide the fact that they are gay). Who is real? It is disheartening to discover saints that ain't. Not judgmental, but there are reasonable expectations from one who declares the Gospel.

Also, it is very difficult to enjoy adult level entertainment without the infusion of worldly acts in movies, comic routines, and concerts. Seeds of immorality are planted. On the other hand, if you only see a person in church, do you really get to know them?

Dr. Sam: *What is the goal of the singles ministry at your church?*

Rita: The Friendship Missionary Baptist Church singles ministry is purposed to approach each project and event of their lives with the Body of Christ in mind. The singles ministry is open to suggestions from other singles who are seeking a holistic and healthy lifestyle in relationships. The Singles Ministry provides support to the now widowed and divorced singles, and single parents through activities and group discussions. The singles ministry is for the never married, divorced, single parent, and widowed, age twenty-five and up. Its mission is to provide support, prayer, and encouragement. To be a ministry that identifies with others and focuses on and gives detailed attention to individual problems by way of discussion and counseling.

Dr. Sam: *Why don't more churches have singles ministries, in your opinion?*

Rita: Singles ministries are lacking because very few men participate. Men don't participate because they are overwhelmed by the women who are specifically looking for a man.

Dr. Sam: *What advice would you give someone who is beginning the dating journey?*

Rita: Take it slow. Pray for divine guidance. Know what you want and don't settle. Consider yourself special and a gift.

Dr. Sam: *How do you feel about dating members of your church?*

Rita: I think this would definitely have an extreme impact on the intimacy question. A relationship with a church member would need to be handled with care as you are not simply dealing with a physical relationship but a spiritual relationship as well. However, equally yoked souls can be the starting point of a lasting relationship.

Approximately twenty individuals including two men from the singles ministry at the Friendship Missionary Baptist Church joined me to discuss dating in the twenty-first century. I started off our discussion by providing the group with an overview of what the book would cover, and then I opened the floor up for general discussion.

Dr. Sam: *How do you feel about online dating?*

Janice: I am very skeptical about meeting people online because I had a situation involving a man I met after I visited one web page and when I visited another web page I realized that the gentleman I'd met on the first website was the same man I met on the second webpage! I guess there is nothing wrong with that, but I was shocked when I realized this person was obviously surfing these websites for fun. He was not serious about a relationship, and when I told him that I had met him previously on another site, he seemed surprised. He was actually using a different name and the only reason I realized it was the same person is because he was using the same basic demographic information. I would imagine that online dating works for some people but this experience really turned me off.

Susan: I am not a fan of online dating. I just don't think people tell the truth, and I have problems trusting what they say.

Janice: I think online dating is fine if you know how to use it. What I mean is you must understand that it is only a tool, but not something that you should use exclusively. I think that it is important to do your research about the site by talking with the Better Business Bureau and checking references.

Dr. Sam: *When do you realize that a person is or is not "the one"?*

Carol: Praying together with a person helps me to realize whether a person could be the one. It's not the process of prayer because a lot of people can pretend that they are walking close with the Lord and say the right things during a prayer, but it is whether they seem to have a praying spirit and if their prayer life matches their Christian walk. That is what I am looking for

Joan: I will be honest with you. If he does not smell right, look right, and sound right then I am probably moving on. I am not saying that he needs to wear designer jeans or look like someone who is posing for *GQ* magazine, but he needs to be well-groomed and simply have something to say. Does that make sense?

Susan: One of the problems with finding "the one" is that there just are not that many available men. If they are not married, they're too old and in poor health or just simply someone you don't click with. You know what I mean?

Dr. Sam: *What advice would you give a Christian who is single and is beginning to date? (Besides telling them to purchase my book! I'm kidding.)*

Nancy: To not place a lot of pressure on themselves to date in the first place. I mean you need to be very comfortable with who you are and not fall into that trap of dating someone just to be dating them.

Samuel H. Hancock Ed.D.

Dr. Sam: *After you start dating a person, when do the problems begin to surface?*

Jane: After you move past the physical attraction.

Mary: When the issue of money comes up.

Cynthia: Children. If you have any, usually you can tell right away if he is a keeper.

Carolyn: When you start observing the baggage from a previous relationship.

Chapter VIII

Sex Complicates Relationships

I think most of us would agree that old habits really do die hard. One of the reasons a person may be somewhat liberal in their view of touching and not as concerned about the ramifications of such behavior is because they habitually have allowed their hands to roam. Depending on what generation you were born into, a wide variety of opinions exist about this very important and sensitive area of interpersonal relationships. For example, if you are a baby-boomer, chances are you probably did not have any conversations with your parents about touching during the dating process. Why? Because most parents in that generation simply did not discuss it with their children. In addition, television programs such as *Happy Days*, *My Three sons*, *Leave It to Beaver*, and *The Partridge Family* certainly did not deal with this sensitive topic.

Although during the sixties, thousands of baby boomers were at Woodstock (a three-day drug-filled rock concert on a farm in New York State), and a large percentage of students on college campuses seemed to have an "anything goes" attitude, the media overall was not as graphic in dealing with issues like drugs and sex. Parents felt that those who were of a "Woodstock mentality" were the exception and not the rule. However, if you were born during the millennial time period, the explosion of technology, pornography, and relaxed attitudes about intimacy that started in the sixties has exposed millennials to subject matter that the baby boomers could never have imagined. But as Christians, "we are in the world but not of the world" (John 17:16). It is very important to understand that the person you are dating is probably a product of the generation he or she was born in, and that his or her attitudes about touching are probably reflective of that generation.

When I became a widower in 2006, as far as my family members, friends (particularly the men), acquaintances, and colleagues were concerned, I was in a very good place. I was in good health, earning a very nice salary, and all my children were adults, employed, and living in their own homes. Two were married. One of my children said, "Dad, you are at a time in your life when you should just have fun and enjoy yourself." The problem was that I did not really know how to enjoy myself, and I did not know how to have fun. Although I enjoyed watching movies, going to plays, bowling, eating out, traveling, and watching sporting events, these activities did not result in the same kind of joy that they had in the past. As a result, I felt very empty while participating in these activities.

At the time I did not realize that I was not only still grieving, but I was a single man with a married man's habits who felt very alone. I was accustomed to having a partner, a significant other, someone with whom I could enjoy activities. I had always been a very selfless, outgoing extrovert, and over time I realized that I enjoyed watching my partner enjoy an activity or event as much as I enjoyed the event myself. That was simply the kind of person I was and still am. Yet I was not really aware that being that kind of person made me very vulnerable in the dating world. I did not understand that my kindness would be taken as a weakness. My self-awareness was very low. Contrary to the way a significant number of single men looked at the single life, I was not interested at all in dating and chasing women and sex. In addition, going clubbing and partying had lost its allure before I married Lorraine back in the mid-seventies. At that time God had spoken to me through the Holy Spirit that it was time for me to consecrate my life to Christ. Therefore, when I found myself single again, I had no desire to change the Christ-focused life that I had led for the past three decades.

I was very fearful about the possibility of relationships going bad. Not only was I afraid of dishonoring my Lord and Savior but, on a more practical note, I was fearful of AIDS and other sexually transmitted diseases, and really concerned about the possibility of a woman developing an unhealthy dependency (i.e. fixation) on me that would be very difficult to break. Please don't misunderstand me. I didn't consider myself to be a Denzel Washington lookalike, but I was acutely aware of the message that sexual intercourse with a woman would send. I knew that if I had had sex with a woman with no regard for how the experience could impact her emotionally, I would pay the price for it (Romans 6:23).

One young lady I spent some time with made it very clear that she wanted to have sex with me. We had gone out to dinner (sound familiar?), the movies, and had become friends. I told her that I was celibate and that, in addition, I felt if we had had sexual intercourse, it would have complicated our relationship. Sexual sin is like no other because it cuts deeper and leaves a much more noticeable scar. When we sin sexually, we sin against our true self. She initially disagreed, but after she had given it some thought and a few more discussions, she agreed.

Let me give you an example. Ladies and gentleman, remember when you were a bit younger and you went through your "oh, he's sooooooo cute" and "she's so fine" stage? Remember your momma warning you (gentlemen) about certain kinds of girls you should stay away from? Or your daddy (ladies) telling you about boys wanting "just one thing?" Remember how you just rolled your eyes, ignored the warnings, and walked away? Your mom and dad had three things you lacked as an adolescent: objectivity, wisdom, and experience. The first two can best be described as "clarity." Your parents were not stirred emotionally by the boys who kept skateboarding in front of your house or the girls who parade by, sometimes ten or fifteen times a day. (They must have been in great physical condition.) The point is that both had lived long enough to know that when one is emotionally or romantically involved with a girl or boy, they lack clarity. That is what the young lady I referred to earlier lacked initially. If we had become sexually involved, we would have lost our objectivity and missed the moment of clarity we needed.

Some of you who are reading this book are thinking, "Yeah, Dr. Sam, it's easy for you to talk about celibacy, clarity, and refraining from sexual intercourse until you're married, because you *are* married. Aren't you being just a little unrealistic on this? I am a Christian and I know a whole bunch of folks who had sex before they married—with the one they married and with others—and are doing just fine. Most are Christians. What's the big deal?"

I understand what you are saying. But whether I am married or single, my Christian brother or sister, the message does not change. These bodies are not ours to do as we please. Our body is the temple of the Holy Spirit (I Corinthians 6:19-20). When we are in the grips of sin, it is impossible to hear God. When the Apostle Paul tells you to grieve not the Holy Spirit (Ephesians 4:30), he is warning you not to suppress the ability of the Holy Spirit to work with you and help you control sinful urges.

It's like the little boy who dove into a quarry for a short swim. When his mother saw him dive, she also spotted an alligator swimming toward him. She became terrified and ran to tell her son that an alligator was swimming directly toward him. When the little boy saw the alligator, he started swimming back, but the alligator reached him before he could swim to safety. His mother reached him at the same time, and a tug of war began. His mother was pulling him in one direction and the alligator was pulling him in the other. His mother was pulling him so hard and holding on so tight that she dug her finger nails into his arm. Finally, a man who was driving by saw what was happening, got his shotgun, and killed the alligator.

The little boy made a miraculous recovery. While he lay in his hospital bed, a reporter from a local newspaper marveled at the fact that, despite the horrible scars on the little boy's legs, he had survived the attack. The little boy turned to the reporter and said, "Yeah, they do look bad, but they will serve as a constant reminder of how blessed I am. However, the scars I am most proud of are the ones that my mother made with her fingernails because she would not let go."

That is how God deals with you when you find yourself in Satan's grasp and can't get away. When you swim out into the dangerous waters of life, due to your lack of understanding, the waters are more dangerous than you thought. God is holding onto you and won't let you go if you trust him. Some of those painful memories that the scars of life have created become a part of our testimony and provide a way to avoid diving into dangerous waters. (I Corinthians 10:13).

The thought of intimacy with a woman was the last thing on my mind after I became a widower. I felt like I was still married, and I had not dated anyone, other than my wife, in over thirty years. As a result, I really didn't know what to do. However, "not touching" was an area that was very important to me because I knew that willfully sinning in general—and sexual sin in particular—would make it impossible for me to hear what the Holy Spirit was trying to tell me and to adhere to its guidance. In addition, as a Christian man trying to live a holy life, I knew that duplicity would make me a hypocrite, and I had a real desire to walk as close to the Lord as I possibly could.

Another of my biggest concerns that developed primarily after I started dating was that most of my Christian (and non-Christian) sisters that I dated had been deeply hurt by other men. I could see it in their eyes, and I could hear it in their voices as we discussed their experiences. I had no desire to inflict more pain on these women, and I knew that it all started with touching. I dated a woman who shared with me that she had dated a married man for eleven years thinking that he would leave his wife and marry her. He never did and she was devastated. She talked about how she had wasted over a decade of her life. I think it is important to focus on the non-physical parts of the relationship and other aspects of a person's life before any touching begins.

The following are some tips I offer to help you on your journey:

- Devoting time to individuals who are serious about the Christian life or who at least understand the kinds of problems uncontrolled touching can create is essential. As Rita said, "Stay away from the 'Saints that ain't.' If you and the person you are dating are on the same page spiritually, you can help each other. If not, you and the young lady or man you are dating will be working at cross purposes and going in different directions.

- Stay in the word of God by laboring in doctrine, seeking the kingdom of God (Matthew 6:33), consistently discussing how each of you are working toward reckoning that old man dead (Romans 6:6; Ephesians 2:1) and having on-going discussions about God's word and how to apply it to your lives.

- Attending church together as much as possible on a regular basis is essential. Staying in touch with other saints by fellowshipping with them, participating in church activities, and talking with your pastor or another person of God who can give you good spiritual direction will help you to stay rooted and grounded.

- When you are alone with this special person, treat her like she is special and keep your hands above her shoulders, never below. I know this is hard. But ladies (and men, there are some aggressive women out there), don't miss this. A man or woman will only go as far as you let him or her. Christian women and men who get the most respect are the ones who know where to draw the line and make it clear that they don't want it crossed. It is crucial that both parties agree that celibacy is important in the relationship.

- Refrain from watching sexually explicit movies or listening to music with provocative lyrics. It is important to protect your mind and your spirit.

- When you go out with a woman or a man for the first several times, try to stay away from settings that may be viewed as romantic. Some women may consider a dinner date as an invitation for a serious relationship, and may fantasize or sincerely believe that the man wants a serious relationship when he doesn't think anything of the setting. He may simply be hungry, and there is no guarantee that he will call her again. Women look at these things a little differently from men.

Chapter IX

Entering into Marriage: What to Consider?

Should every person who is single marry? Marriage is not a rite of passage to womanhood or manhood. Marriage is a calling from God. Marriage may be consistent with God's divine plan for your life, but a call to marriage is a serious matter. A call to marriage is an inner urge, a strong directive to marry. It should be undertaken with much thoughtfulness. Persons seeking marriage should first consult with God to determine if this is truly an urge or a "call" or simply a carnal desire to marry a person for a multitude of reasons. You must be certain and knowledgeable of what marriage entails prior to making a sincere commitment to a partner. A call to marriage is independent and has very little to do with the number of years you have invested in the relationship. For example, just because you have dated for four years does not mean you automatically have a call to marriage with *that* person. Just because you are getting older and your childbearing years are fading does not mean that there is a call to marriage. Just because you are a forty-year-old man living at home with your mother does not mean you have a call to marry. God created Eve from Adam. Adam did not ask for or seek Eve (Genesis 2:21).

A call to marriage requires that you consider other people who are involved in your life (children, siblings, parents, grandparents, close friends), as they can contribute to the success or failure of your marriage. A call to marriage must be a spirit-filled one in which

God has anointed the chosen relationship. Following the call to marriage, Christian counseling is advised until the relationship is considered satisfactory and God-centered in nature. It is a blessing to be single and perfectly fine to stay single if you sincerely believe and are convinced after seeking guidance from God that being single is God's will for you. Matthew 6:17-24 charges you to have spiritual vision, which is your capacity to see the world from God's point of view. But self-serving desires, interests, and goals can block that vision. Serving God is the only way to restore it. A pure eye is one that is fixed on God. Some of you can see yourselves being successful as a wife or husband, but not as a single person.

Chapter X

Conclusion

I would like to take this opportunity to thank you for taking the time to have this conversation with me about dating in the twenty-first century. I hope and pray that you have been challenged, inspired, motivated, informed, and encouraged to keep the faith. God will supply your every need and he will never leave or forsake you. I don't consider myself an expert in the dating arena, and you may not agree with my opinions, conclusions, or recommendations. However, all of you are experts in your own experiences, and my story and the things I have discussed are my interpretations of my experiences. I am not perfect, Kattie and I are not perfect, and our marriage is not perfect. My first marriage was not perfect. There are no perfect marriages or relationships. They take work, and I am working on being the best husband I can be every day. Please remember that if two people can become friends, especially best friends, that is the foundation for a successful marriage, if marriage is what you are looking for.

If you experience pain, frustration, confusion, or disappointment, don't panic. Try to embrace it as "all things do work together for good to them that love God and are called according to his purpose" (Romans 8:28).

References

PREFACE

Nader, R. (1965). *Unsafe at Any Speed* Published: Richard Grossman

Chapter I

King James Version of the Bible Large Print (New Open Bible) KJVOP

United States Government: Operated by the United State Air Force *Global Positioning System* (Launched in February 1978)

Matthew 6:33 KJVOB Page 1123

Dack, R. (2013). Ten Ways to Tame First Date Anxiety *Dating Tips* (*Https://www.eharmony.com/dating-advice/dating* tips/

Job 31:1 KJVOB Page 609

Romans 6:11 KJVOB Page 1331

Ephesians 5:1 KJVOB Page 1391

Philippians 1:27 KJVOB Page 1400

Excerpt from sermon preached in April 2007 (H.A.L.T). at Atlanta First Baptist Church by Charles Stanley

Lee, M (2016). Here's how 770 Pastors Describe Their Struggle with Porn (The Barna Research Group)

Ephesians 5:18 KJVOB Page 1391

Ephesians 4:1 KJVOB Page 1390

Romans 12:2 KJVOB Page 1337

Hosea 14:9 KJVOB Page 1005

Chapter II

Philippians 3:14 KJVOB Page 1401

Belong, Value, Competent Crabb, L., (1977). *Effective Biblical Counseling* Ministry Resources Library

Vernon, V. A., (2011). *10 Rules of Dating* Shaker Heights Ohio: Victory Media & Publishing Company.

Proverbs 3:6 KJVOB Page 715

The Toledo Blade Charles Shultz creator of Peanuts "Resisting Change" Published in May 2016

II Timothy 1:7 KJVOB Page 1433

Genesis 37:1-11 KJVOB Page 49

Genesis 37:18-29 KJVOB Page 49

Genesis 37:3 KJVOB Page 49

Genesis 50:19, 20 KJVOBPage 64

Chapter III

Philippians 2:13 KJVOB Page 1400

Romans 12:1-2 KJVOB Page 1337

Proverbs 3:5-6 KJOVB Page 715

Hebrews 10:25 KJOVB Page 1458

Exodus 33:7-11 KJOVB Page 106

Ephesians 6:12 KJVOB Page 1393

Psalm 30:5 KJVOB Page 641

I Kings 19:3-4 KJVOB Page 418

Psalm 31:9-12 KJVOB Page 641

Jeremiah 1:19 KJVOB Page 844

Jeremiah 16:1-2 KJVOB Page 862

Exodus 33:7 KJVOB Page 106

Exodus 33:8 KJVOB Page 106

Exodus 33:10.11 KJVOB Page 106

Matthew 26:36-46 KJVOB Page 1150 & 1151

Psalm 3:3 KJVOB Page 626

Psalm 139:7-8 KJVOB Page 704

I Timothy 3:15 KJVOB Page 1436

Ephesians 4:14 KJVOB Page 1390

Chapter IV

++Movie *The Intern* Warner Brothers released September 15, 2015

Judges 16:19 KJVOB Page 303

Judges 14:3 KJVOB Page 302

II Cor 5:7 KJVOB Page 1368

Galatians 6:7 KJVOB Page 1383

Genesis 2:18 KJVOB Page 7

Eccl 4:10-11 KJVOB Page 753

Proverbs 1:7 KJVOP Page 714

I Cor 14:40 KJVOB Page 1358

I Cor 14:33 KJVOB Page 1358

I Cor 6;19 KJVOB Page 1351

Galatians 6:7 KJVOB Page 1383

Romans 6:23 KJVOB Page 1331

Genesis 3:5 KJVOB Page 9

Ephesians 4:14 KJVOB Page 1390

Psalm 139 KJVOB Page 704-705

Ephesians 6:4b KJVOB Page 1392

Proverbs 17:6 KJVOB Page 729

Luke 16:1-8 KJVOB Page 1218

Evans. T (1984) *Tony Evans Book of Illustrations* Moody Publishers: Chicago Illinois

Verification: Williams, P. M. F., & Williams, R. D., (2005). *Single Wisdom*: RP Publishing

Chapter V

Romans 12:2 KJVOB Page 1337

John 15:3-5 KJVOB Page 1258-59

Romans 7:15 KJVOB Page 1332

Film *How to be Single* Warner Brothers Pictures released February 12, 2016

Chapter VI

Internet Flirt Sites

Philippians 2:13 KJVOB Page 1400

Romans 12:10 KJVOB Page 1337

Matthew 27:34 KJVOB Page 1229

Philippians 4:7 KJVOB Page 1402

Romans 6:23 KJVOB Page 1331

Chapter VII

Singles Ministry Friendship Baptist Church Columbus Ohio (Session held in June of 2016 at Friendship Baptist Church)

Chapter VIII

John 17:16 KJVOB Page 1262

Romans 6:23 KJVOB Page 1331

Cor 6:19-20 KJVOB Page 1351

Ephesians 4:30 KJVOB Page 1391

Alligator Story Indiana Missionary Baptist Church Newsletter

I Cor 10:13 KJVOB Page 1354

Matthew 6:33 KJVOB Page 1123

Romans 6:6 KJVOB Page 1329

Ephesians 2:1 KJVOB Page 1387

Chapter IX

Genesis 2:21 KJVOB Page 8

Matthew 6:17-24 KJVOB Page 1123

Romans 8:28 KJVOB Page 1333

Printed in the United States
By Bookmasters